Cooking Light.

STIR-FRY

COOKBOOK

Cooking Light.

STIR-FRY
COOKBOOK

COMPILED AND EDITED BY
SUSAN M. MCINTOSH, M.S., R.D.

ISBN: 0-8487-2707-x
Printed in the United States of America
First Printing 2002

Previously published as *Low-Fat Ways to Stir-Fry*
  © 1996 by Oxmoor House, Inc.

Editor-in-Chief: Nancy Fitzpatrick Wyatt
Editorial Director, Special Interest Publications: Ann H. Harvey
Senior Foods Editor: Katherine M. Eakin
Senior Editor, Editorial Services: Olivia Kindig Wells
Art Director: James Boone

COOKING LIGHT₀ STIR-FRY COOKBOOK

Menu and Recipe Consultant: Susan McEwen McIntosh, M.S., R.D.
Assistant Editor: Kelly Hooper Troiano
Associate Foods Editor: Anne Chappell Cain, M.S., M.P.H., R.D.
Copy Editor: Shari K. Wimberly
Editorial Assistant: Kaye Howard Smith
Indexer: Mary Ann Laurens
Associate Art Director: Cynthia R. Cooper
Designer: Carol Damsky
Senior Photographer: Jim Bathie
Photographers: Howard L. Puckett, Ralph Anderson
Senior Photo Stylist: Kay E. Clarke
Photo Stylists: Cindy Manning Barr, Virginia R. Cravens
Production and Distribution Director: Phillip Lee
Associate Production Manager: Vanessa Cobbs Richardson
Production Assistant: Valerie L. Heard

Cover: *Teriyaki Beef and Broccoli (recipe on page 57)*
Frontispiece: *Sweet-and-Sour Shrimp in Fruit Sauce (recipe on page 45)*

To order additional publications, call 1-800-633-4910.

**For more books to enrich your life, visit
oxmoorhouse.com**

CONTENTS

STIR UP FLAVOR!

Stir-frying originated centuries ago in China, where meals had to be cooked quickly and efficiently because fuel for cooking was scarce. Today, stir-frying is the perfect answer for busy, health-conscious cooks who want to prepare nutritious, low-fat meals in a hurry.

Like its name implies, stir-frying involves cooking food over high heat and constantly stirring or tossing the food as it cooks. But unlike most fried foods, stir-fries can be prepared without much fat or oil. And since the food cooks quickly, more vitamins and minerals are preserved.

Stir-frying in a nonstick wok with a nonmetal spoon

Although the term "stir-fry" usually brings to mind Oriental mixtures served over rice, you can stir-fry foods from other cuisines as well. From the filling for a Tex-Mex fajita to an Italian-seasoned meat to serve with pasta, the possibilities are limitless.

Whether you're a longtime pro at stir-frying or a novice with this method of cooking, this book is for you. Read on for recommended ingredients and techniques that will help you stir up some of the healthiest and tastiest of entrées and side dishes.

WHAT YOU NEED

Stir-fries are typically prepared in an Oriental wok. Its classic rounded shape makes it perfect for stir-frying. The deep, sloping sides and rounded bottom allow food to cook evenly and quickly. But, if you prefer, you can use a large skillet, stir-fry pan, or sauté pan for most of the recipes.

There are two basic types of woks. The traditional round-bottomed wok (accompanied with a ring stand) is recommended for cooking over a gas flame. A flat-bottomed wok can be used over electric or gas cooktops. No ring stand is necessary with this type of wok because the flat bottom allows the wok to sit directly on the heating element.

A wok for stir-frying should be made of a material that is a good conductor of heat, such as carbon steel or aluminum. Stainless steel woks are also available; some manufacturers combine stainless steel with aluminum or copper to improve the material's ability to conduct heat.

Carbon steel woks come from the factory with a coating that should be removed before first use. (Follow the manufacturer's directions about how to remove the coating.) The clean, dry wok should be rubbed with oil before first use and after each use.

A frequently used steel wok that is cleaned and oiled properly will become "seasoned" and develop its own natural nonstick coating. Never scrub a seasoned wok or put it in the dishwasher. Instead, just as for a seasoned, well-used cast-iron skillet, wash the wok with warm water only, not soap, and dry it thoroughly before storing. Store seasoned woks in a well-ventilated area to prevent the oil on the surface of the wok from turning rancid.

Aluminum and stainless steel woks require little care. They should simply be washed in hot soapy water after each use. An occasional rubbing with oil may be recommended.

Electric woks are also available, usually with a nonstick surface. Follow the manufacturer's directions for using and cleaning electric woks.

Although the wok is considered the traditional pan for stir-frying, a large, deep skillet or sauté pan works as well. The key is to use a pan that is large enough and deep enough to allow plenty of room for tossing the food while it cooks.

We generally recommend a heavy 12-inch skillet. (If you are using a lightweight skillet, you'll need to be careful while stir-frying; food tends to scorch at high temperatures in lightweight cookware.)

Whether you are using a wok or skillet, you will be able to cook with less oil if the pan has a nonstick surface. The use of vegetable cooking spray is often recommended, even with a nonstick surface.

Spraying skillet with cooking spray

You will find many accessories available for stir-frying, but all you will really need is a long-handled spoon or spatula for stirring the food, a good knife, and a cutting board. If your wok or skillet has a nonstick surface, use wooden, plastic, or coated utensils instead of metal to keep from chipping the nonstick surface. Because most stir-fries call for thinly sliced meat and vegetables, you will need a sharp knife and a cutting board to prepare your ingredients for stir-frying. A high-quality knife will make the job easier.

Using a sharp knife to slice vegetables

KNIFE SELECTION

An excellent knife can make quick work of food preparation. Quality can vary among knives, so it is best to base your purchase on workmanship and the blade's alloy content.

For high-quality workmanship, look for a tempered blade, which makes the knife more durable, and a long tang, which is a portion of the blade that runs through the handle. An inexpensive knife has a short tang, increasing the chance that the blade and handle will separate. The handle should be made of a material that's a poor conductor of heat, such as wood or a wood and plastic combination.

Below are descriptions of blade alloy content.

Types	Advantages	Disadvantages
Carbon Steel	Sharpest edge; chef's choice	Rusts if not immediately dried after use; stains when left in contact with acidic foods
High-Carbon Stainless Steel	Will not rust or stain; good for humid climates	Most expensive; not as sharp as carbon steel
Stainless Steel	Resists rust and stains	Dull blade but sharper than superstainless
Superstainless Steel	Resists rust and stains	Dullest blade; cannot be sharpened

THE KEY INGREDIENTS

You will already have many of the basic stir-fry ingredients on hand. However, some of the typical sauces and seasonings are more unusual. These ingredients are definitely worth seeking out in the ethnic section of your supermarket.

Clockwise from left: *Chili puree with garlic, dark sesame oil, fish sauce, hoisin sauce, and rice noodles*

Asian noodles used in some stir-fries include rice noodles, cellophane noodles (bean threads), harusame, soba, somen, and ramen. These noodles cook quickly and soak up the flavor of anything you pour over them.

Bamboo shoots are available fresh in some Oriental markets, although canned bamboo shoots are most commonly used.

Chili puree with garlic adds heat and flavor to stir-fries, even when just a spoonful is added.

Cornstarch is commonly used to thicken sauces for stir-fries. Cornstarch should be mixed well with a small amount of cold liquid before it is added to a hot mixture to prevent lumps from forming.

Fish sauce has a salty flavor and is the "secret" ingredient in many Asian recipes. A little bit goes a long way.

Garlic is available fresh in the produce section of the supermarket. Bottled minced fresh garlic is a convenient option.

Gingerroot is a knobby, brown spice that has an extraordinary hot and spicy flavor. Choose thick pieces with smooth skin; they can be peeled easily with a vegetable peeler and then grated or minced. Ground ginger is also available and recommended for many Oriental marinades and sauces.

Hoisin sauce, often referred to as Peking sauce, has a sweet-and-spicy flavor that enriches stir-fries, pastas, and marinades.

Oil is recommended for most stir-fries to prevent sticking. If cooking in a well-seasoned or nonstick wok or skillet, you'll need very little.

When you do need oil, use one that is light in texture and flavor and can withstand high heat. Peanut oil is traditionally used for stir-frying because it does not smoke at high temperatures. But canola, corn, or soybean oils are fine to use. Pure (virgin) olive oil is better for stir-frying than deeper-colored, extra virgin olive oil.

Some recipes call for flavored oils such as sesame and chili. Even in small quantities of 1 teaspoon or less, they add a robust flavor to stir-fries.

Oyster sauce, a flavorful, thick, dark brown sauce, adds richness to many Oriental dishes.

Rice is classified according to its size—short-, medium-, or long-grain. Short-grain rice is short, plump, and very moist when cooked. It sticks together more than long-grain varieties and is often preferred for Oriental food because it is easiest to eat with chopsticks.

Rice vinegar is made from either fermented rice or rice wine. It is mainly used in Oriental cooking and can be found with other vinegars or in the Oriental food section of the supermarket.

Soy sauce is common to Oriental stir-fries and is also used in soups, marinades, sauces, and vegetable dishes. Regular soy sauce is high in sodium, but reduced-sodium varieties are also available.

Vegetable cooking spray is essential for low-fat cooking. One of the best ways to decrease the amount of fat in stir-fries is to coat the inside of your wok or skillet with cooking spray before adding the oil. The cooking spray maximizes the effectiveness of the small amounts of oil recommended.

Water chestnuts add a crunchy texture to Oriental stir-fries and many salads and vegetable side dishes. They are readily available canned, although some people prefer fresh water chestnuts, which can be found in Oriental markets.

CUTTING TECHNIQUES

Cutting ingredients correctly is important for successful stir-fries. Mastering the techniques pictured below will ensure that cut foods that are added to a recipe will cook in the time specified. To make cutting easier, begin with a sharp set of knives and a cutting board. (See page 7 for information about purchasing good-quality knives.)

Cube. *Cut food into ¹/₂-inch blocks.*

Mince. *Cut food into very small, irregular-shaped pieces.*

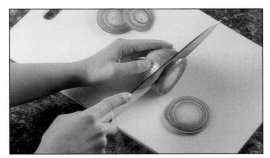

Slice. *Hold food with fingers away from blade at a distance that equals one slice.*

Dice. *Cut food into cubes that measure ¹/₈ to ¹/₄ inch on each side.*

Diagonally slice. *Cut food by holding the knife at a 45-degree angle to the food.*

Chop. *Cut food into ¹/₄-inch irregular-shaped pieces (about the size of an English pea).*

Julienne. *Cut food into ¹/₈-inch-thick slices; stack, and cut into ¹/₈-inch-thick strips.*

STIR-FRY SUCCESS

Stir-frying is a fast method of cooking. To make it successful, be sure to read the entire recipe and prepare ingredients before heating the wok. Once the wok is hot, you won't have time to stop and slice the vegetables and meat.

Here are some tips to remember:

• Have all the ingredients sliced, measured, and ready to go before you turn on the heat. Line up ingredients as needed near the wok. Don't forget to assemble any sauces, such as a cornstarch sauce, before starting.

• Plan to start cooking the rice, if needed, before you begin the stir-fry. It will be cooked and hot when the stir-fry is ready.

• Make sure the vegetables are cut into uniform pieces (approximately the same size and shape) so that they all will get done at the same time.

• Slice meat and chicken thinly so that they will cook quickly. For easier slicing, partially freeze meat before cutting it into thin strips.

Slicing partially frozen meat

• Slice meat and vegetables diagonally to expose more surface area, which allows foods to cook faster and absorb more flavor.

• Use a wok or large, heavy skillet. Cooking spray and small amounts of vegetable oil will keep foods from sticking or burning at high temperatures.

• Add oil to the wok by drizzling it around the top edge of the wok, coating the sides and bottom. You may need to hold the wok by its handles and turn it to swirl the oil so that it coats the entire cooking surface.

• Heat vegetable cooking spray and/or oil in the wok or skillet until hot. Preheating the wok before adding ingredients is vital to crisp-tender vegetables and seared meats. When food is added, it should sizzle on contact.

• Stir-fry the garlic, gingerroot, and onion first to season the oil in most recipes.

• Pat foods dry with a paper towel before adding to the wok or skillet to avoid spattering.

• Cook in small batches. Overloading the wok or skillet will lower the heat and result in soggy food.

• Adjust the cooking temperature from time to time so that the temperature of the oil remains constant. The oil should be hot but not smoking. If the heat is not high enough, the food will be steamed instead of seared.

• Stir constantly for even cooking and to prevent sticking. Use wok utensils or wooden spoons to stir or toss ingredients.

• Adjust cooking times as necessary since the various types of cookware transport heat differently.

• Be careful not to overcook meat. Stir-fry only until it loses its pink color.

• Stir-fry the firmest vegetables first. Then add tender vegetables that require little cooking. Stir-fry only until the vegetables are crisp-tender to keep colors vibrant and nutrition high.

• Push food up the side if too much liquid accumulates. Cook until liquid evaporates.

• Stir the cornstarch sauce again before adding it to the wok or skillet because cornstarch tends to settle to the bottom.

Adding cornstarch mixture to cooked meat and vegetables

LOW-FAT BASICS

*W*hether you are trying to lose or maintain weight, low-fat eating makes good sense. Research studies show that decreasing your fat intake reduces risks of heart disease, diabetes, and some types of cancer. The goal recommended by major health groups is an intake of 30 percent or less of total daily calories from fat.

The *Cooking Light Stir-Fry Cookbook* helps you meet that goal. It gives you practical, delicious recipes with realistic advice about low-fat cooking and eating. The recipes are lower in total fat than traditional recipes, and most provide less than 30 percent of calories from fat and less than 10 percent from saturated fat.

If you have one high-fat item during a meal, you can balance it with low-fat choices for the rest of the day and still remain within the recommended percentage. For example, fat contributes 42 percent of the calories in Almond-Topped Peaches for the Dinner from the Wok menu beginning on page 17. However, because the dessert is combined with other low-fat foods, the total menu provides only 19 percent of calories as fat.

The goal of fat reduction is not to eliminate fat entirely. In fact, some fat is needed to transport fat-soluble vitamins and maintain other body functions.

FIGURING THE FAT

The easiest way to achieve a diet with 30 percent or fewer of total calories from fat is to establish a daily "fat budget" based on the total number of calories you need each day. Multiply your current weight by 15 to estimate your daily calorie requirements. Remember that calorie requirements vary according to age, body size, and level of activity. To gain or lose 1 pound a week, add or subtract 500 calories a day. (A diet of fewer than 1,200 calories is not recommended unless medically supervised.)

Now calculate your recommended fat allowance by multiplying your daily calorie needs by .30 and dividing by 9 (the number of calories in each gram of fat). Your daily fat gram intake should not exceed this number. For quick reference, see the Daily Fat Limits chart.

DAILY FAT LIMITS		
Calories Per Day	30 Percent of Calories	Grams of Fat
1,200	360	40
1,500	450	50
1,800	540	60
2,000	600	67
2,200	660	73
2,500	750	83
2,800	840	93

NUTRITIONAL ANALYSIS

Each recipe in *Cooking Light Stir-Fry Cookbook* has been kitchen-tested by a staff of qualified home economists. Registered dietitians have determined the nutrient information, using a computer system that analyzes every ingredient. These efforts ensure the success of each recipe and will help you fit these recipes into your own meal planning.

The nutrient grid that follows each recipe provides calories per serving and the percentage of calories from fat. Also, the grid lists the grams of total fat, saturated fat, protein, and carbohydrate, and the milligrams of cholesterol and sodium per serving. The nutrient values are as accurate as possible and are based on these assumptions:

• When the recipe calls for cooked pasta, rice, or noodles, the analysis is based on cooking without additional salt or fat.

• The calculations indicate that meat and poultry are trimmed of fat and skin before cooking.

• Only the amount of marinade absorbed by the food is calculated.

• Garnishes and other optional ingredients are not calculated.

• Some of the alcohol calories evaporate during heating, and only those remaining are calculated.

• When a range is given for an ingredient (3 to 3½ cups, for instance), the lesser amount is calculated.

• Fruits and vegetables listed in the ingredients are not peeled unless specified.

Pork Chow Mein, Couscous with Tomato and Onions, and Gingered Broccoli (menu on page 20)

SENSIBLE DINNERS

*D*o you want to prepare great meals for your family and friends without spending hours in the kitchen? Then try stir-frying. This quick and healthy cooking method works well for a variety of foods. And the five menus in this chapter—from traditional Oriental dinners to a vegetarian stir-fry with beans and rice—will get you in and out of the kitchen in a hurry.

Using these menus as guides, you can choose one of the other stir-fry entrées in this book to suit your taste. For example, Beef and Broccoli with Oyster Sauce (page 57) could substitute as the main dish in the Chinese New Year's Dinner Party beginning on page 14. Or you might try Szechuan Shrimp Stir-Fry (page 44) instead of the chicken dish in Dinner from the Wok (page 17). But whatever your pleasure, you'll find that a stir-fry dish is a great low-fat choice.

Chinese New Year's Dinner Party

Here's a menu for Chinese New Year—or any festive occasion.
Start with Shrimp Toast, followed by a tangy salad and gingered
beef. For dessert, offer Almond Moons. (The menu analysis reflects
four appetizers and two cookies per person.)

Shrimp Toast

Orange and Onion Salad

Gingered Beef and Peppers

Almond Moons

Jasmine tea

Serves 6
TOTAL CALORIES PER SERVING: 633
(CALORIES FROM FAT: 18%)

Shrimp Toast

1½ cups water
½ pound unpeeled medium-size fresh shrimp
2 tablespoons finely chopped green onions
2 tablespoons finely chopped sweet red pepper
1 tablespoon chopped fresh cilantro
2 tablespoons low-sodium soy sauce
1 teaspoon dark sesame oil
1 egg white, lightly beaten
6 (1-ounce) slices whole wheat bread, toasted

Bring water to a boil; add shrimp, and cook 3 to 5
minutes or until shrimp turn pink. Drain well; rinse
with cold water. Peel and devein shrimp.

Position knife blade in food processor bowl; add
shrimp. Process until shrimp are finely chopped.

Combine shrimp, green onions, and next 4 ingredients in a medium bowl. Add egg white, stirring well.

Trim crusts from bread slices, and cut each slice
into 4 triangles. Spread shrimp mixture evenly over
bread triangles; place triangles on a large baking sheet.

Bake at 350° for 8 minutes or until thoroughly
heated and lightly browned. Yield: 24 appetizers.

PER APPETIZER: 25 CALORIES (18% FROM FAT)
FAT 0.5G (SATURATED FAT 0.1G)
PROTEIN 1.9G CARBOHYDRATE 3.5G
CHOLESTEROL 9MG SODIUM 83MG

Orange and Onion Salad

*Dark sesame oil adds an intense nutty flavor—a
little goes a long way.*

2 tablespoons rice wine vinegar
2 tablespoons low-sodium soy sauce
2 teaspoons dark sesame oil
¼ teaspoon grated orange rind
2 large oranges, peeled, seeded, and sliced
1 small purple onion, thinly sliced
3 cups torn red leaf lettuce

Combine first 4 ingredients in a small bowl, stirring with a wire whisk. Arrange orange and onion in
a 13- x 9- x 2-inch dish. Pour vinegar mixture over
orange and onion. Cover and chill 30 minutes.

Place lettuce evenly on individual salad plates.
Arrange orange and onion slices over lettuce, using
a slotted spoon. Drizzle vinegar mixture evenly
over salads. Yield: 6 servings.

PER SERVING: 42 CALORIES (34% FROM FAT)
FAT 1.6G (SATURATED FAT 0.2G)
PROTEIN 0.7G CARBOHYDRATE 6.1G
CHOLESTEROL 0MG SODIUM 132MG

Gingered Beef and Peppers

GINGERED BEEF AND PEPPERS

1 pound lean boneless top sirloin steak
¼ cup plus 2 tablespoons low-sodium soy
    sauce
1½ tablespoons peeled, minced gingerroot
¼ teaspoon dried crushed red pepper
4 cloves garlic, minced
1½ cups canned no-salt-added beef broth,
    undiluted
2 tablespoons plus 2 teaspoons cornstarch
Vegetable cooking spray
2 teaspoons peanut oil, divided
1 cup julienne-sliced sweet red pepper
1 cup julienne-sliced sweet yellow pepper
1½ cups snow pea pods, trimmed
3 green onions, diagonally sliced into ½-inch
    pieces
6 cups cooked rice (cooked without salt or fat)
Green onion curls (optional)

Trim fat from steak; slice steak diagonally across grain into ⅛-inch-wide strips. Cut strips crosswise into 1½-inch-long pieces. Combine soy sauce and next 3 ingredients in a heavy-duty, zip-top plastic bag. Add steak; seal bag, and shake until steak is well coated. Marinate in refrigerator at least 8 hours, turning bag occasionally. Drain steak, reserving marinade. Set steak aside.

Combine marinade, beef broth, and cornstarch, stirring well; set aside.

Coat a wok or large nonstick skillet with cooking spray; add 1 teaspoon oil. Heat at medium-high (375°) until hot. Add sweet red pepper, sweet yellow pepper, and snow peas; stir-fry until vegetables are crisp-tender. Remove pepper mixture from wok; set aside.

Add remaining 1 teaspoon oil to wok. Add steak and sliced green onions; stir-fry 5 minutes or to desired degree of doneness. Add pepper mixture, and toss well. Stir marinade mixture with a wire whisk; add to steak mixture. Stir-fry 1 minute or until mixture comes to a boil. Stir-fry 1 additional minute. Serve over rice. Garnish with green onion curls, if desired. Yield: 6 servings.

PER SERVING: 384 CALORIES (14% FROM FAT)
FAT 6.0G (SATURATED FAT 1.7G)
PROTEIN 21.3G CARBOHYDRATE 56.9G
CHOLESTEROL 46MG SODIUM 440MG

ALMOND MOONS

The flavor of Almond Moons is similar to that of fortune cookies, but these cookies are softer and more moist.

2 tablespoons margarine, softened
1 tablespoon almond paste
¼ cup sugar
2 tablespoons frozen egg substitute, thawed
⅛ teaspoon almond extract
¾ cup all-purpose flour
¼ teaspoon baking soda
Dash of salt
2 teaspoons sugar
Vegetable cooking spray

Beat margarine and almond paste at medium speed of an electric mixer until creamy; gradually add ¼ cup sugar, beating well. Add egg substitute and almond extract; beat well.

Combine flour, baking soda, and salt in a small bowl. Gradually add flour mixture to almond mixture, stirring well. Shape dough into a ball; cover and chill 1 hour.

Divide chilled dough into 10 equal portions. Shape each portion into a ball. Roll balls in 2 teaspoons sugar. Place balls, 4 inches apart, on a cookie sheet coated with cooking spray. Bake at 350° for 9 minutes or until golden. Remove from oven; cut cookies in half. Remove from cookie sheets, and let cool completely on a wire rack. Yield: 20 cookies.

PER COOKIE: 53 CALORIES (24% FROM FAT)
FAT 1.4G (SATURATED FAT 0.2G)
PROTEIN 0.7G CARBOHYDRATE 6.9G
CHOLESTEROL 0MG SODIUM 39MG

DINNER FROM THE WOK

To keep preparation for this quick family meal zipping along, get organized. First, set out all the ingredients you'll need. Then prepare the wonton chips, and toast the almonds for Almond-Topped Peaches. Next, marinate the chicken, and start the rice.

After slicing the pepper and onion, cook Mandarin-Style Snow Peas. Now it's time to heat up the wok and start stir-frying. Go ahead and call in the family—dinner will be ready within minutes. (Menu analysis allows six Sesame Wonton Chips per person.)

Chicken with Hoisin Sauce

Mandarin-Style Snow Peas

Sesame Wonton Chips

Almond-Topped Peaches

Hot tea

Serves 4
TOTAL CALORIES PER SERVING: 598
(CALORIES FROM FAT: 19%)

CHICKEN WITH HOISIN SAUCE

4 (4-ounce) skinned, boned chicken breast
    halves, cut into ½-inch strips
½ cup hoisin sauce
¼ cup water
2 cloves garlic, minced
Vegetable cooking spray
1 teaspoon vegetable oil
½ teaspoon sesame oil
1 medium-size sweet red pepper, cut into
    1-inch pieces
1 large onion, cut into 1-inch pieces
2 cups cooked rice (cooked without salt or fat)

Place chicken in a shallow dish. Combine hoisin sauce, water, and minced garlic in a small bowl. Reserve half of hoisin sauce mixture. Pour remaining mixture over chicken. Cover and marinate in refrigerator at least 15 minutes. Remove chicken from marinade; discard marinade.

Coat a wok or large nonstick skillet with cooking spray; add vegetable and sesame oils. Heat at medium-high (375°) until hot. Add sweet red pepper and onion pieces; stir-fry 3 minutes or until crisp-tender.

Add chicken and reserved hoisin sauce mixture to wok; stir-fry 3 minutes or until chicken is tender. To serve, spoon ½ cup rice onto each of 4 individual serving plates; spoon chicken mixture evenly over rice. Yield: 4 servings.

PER SERVING: 366 CALORIES (15% FROM FAT)
FAT 6.1G (SATURATED FAT 1.5G)
PROTEIN 38.3G   CARBOHYDRATE 36.7G
CHOLESTEROL 96MG   SODIUM 504MG

Chicken with Hoisin Sauce, Sesame Wonton Chips, and Mandarin-Style Snow Peas

MANDARIN-STYLE SNOW PEAS

1 (6-ounce) package frozen snow pea pods,
    thawed
1 (8-ounce) can sliced water chestnuts,
    drained
2 tablespoons dry white wine
1 tablespoon rice wine vinegar
Dash of ground ginger

Cook snow peas in a medium saucepan according to package directions, omitting salt and fat. Drain well. Add water chestnuts and remaining ingredients; stir well. Cook over medium heat until thoroughly heated. Yield: 4 (½-cup) servings.

PER SERVING: 47 CALORIES (2% FROM FAT)
FAT 0.1G (SATURATED FAT 0.2G)
PROTEIN 1.9G   CARBOHYDRATE 10.2G
CHOLESTEROL 0MG   SODIUM 7MG

SESAME WONTON CHIPS

1 egg white, lightly beaten
1 tablespoon low-sodium soy sauce
½ teaspoon garlic powder
⅛ teaspoon ground ginger
12 fresh or frozen wonton skins, thawed
Vegetable cooking spray
1 tablespoon sesame seeds, toasted

Combine first 4 ingredients; set aside. Cut each wonton skin in half diagonally; place in a 15- x 10- x 1-inch jellyroll pan coated with cooking spray. Brush egg white mixture over skins; sprinkle evenly with sesame seeds. Bake at 375° for 6 minutes or until crisp and lightly browned. Remove from pan; let cool completely on wire racks. Yield: 24 chips.

PER CHIP: 15 CALORIES (18% FROM FAT)
FAT 0.3G (SATURATED FAT 0.0G)
PROTEIN 0.6G   CARBOHYDRATE 2.5G
CHOLESTEROL 0MG   SODIUM 41MG

ALMOND-TOPPED PEACHES

¼ cup finely chopped almonds, toasted
2 tablespoons brown sugar
1½ teaspoons lemon juice
2 large ripe peaches, peeled, pitted, and halved
    lengthwise
Fresh mint sprigs (optional)

Combine chopped almonds and brown sugar in a small bowl; stir well, and set aside.
Brush lemon juice over peach halves. Press almond mixture evenly onto rounded side of each peach half. To serve, place in individual dessert bowls, and garnish with fresh mint sprigs, if desired. Yield: 4 servings.

PER SERVING: 93 CALORIES (42% FROM FAT)
FAT 4.3G (SATURATED FAT 0.4G)
PROTEIN 1.9G   CARBOHYDRATE 13.3G
CHOLESTEROL 0MG   SODIUM 4MG

Almond-Topped Peaches

PRE-SYMPHONY SUPPER
(pictured on page 12)

Both the entrée and the vegetable side dish are stir-fried for this
festive supper. Serve with couscous, and finish with a simple dessert.
(The menu analysis includes 6 ounces wine per serving.)

Pork Chow Mein

Couscous with Tomato and Onions

Gingered Broccoli

Fresh Berries with Lemon Cream

Blush wine

Serves 4
TOTAL CALORIES PER SERVING: 642
(CALORIES FROM FAT: 16%)

PORK CHOW MEIN

1 pound lean boneless pork loin, trimmed
1 cup canned no-salt-added chicken broth
¼ cup low-sodium soy sauce
3 tablespoons cornstarch
1 teaspoon ground ginger
Vegetable cooking spray
1 clove garlic, minced
1 cup thinly sliced carrot
1 cup thinly sliced celery
1 cup chopped onion
1 cup coarsely chopped cabbage
1 cup chopped fresh spinach

Slice pork diagonally across grain into 2- x ¼-inch strips. Combine broth and next 3 ingredients; set aside.

Coat a wok or large nonstick skillet with cooking spray; heat at medium-high (375°) until hot. Add pork and garlic; stir-fry 5 minutes. Add carrot and remaining 4 ingredients; stir-fry 3 minutes. Add broth mixture; cover and cook 3 minutes, stirring occasionally. Yield: 4 (1-cup) servings.

PER SERVING: 259 CALORIES (30% FROM FAT)
FAT 8.5G (SATURATED FAT 2.9G)
PROTEIN 26.8G   CARBOHYDRATE 15.5G
CHOLESTEROL 71MG   SODIUM 518MG

COUSCOUS WITH TOMATO AND ONIONS

Vegetable cooking spray
½ teaspoon vegetable oil
¼ cup sliced green onions
¾ cup water
1 teaspoon chicken-flavored bouillon granules
½ cup couscous, uncooked
2 teaspoons low-sodium soy sauce
⅓ cup peeled, seeded, and chopped tomato
1 tablespoon chopped fresh parsley
¼ teaspoon freshly ground pepper

Coat a saucepan with cooking spray; add oil. Place over medium-high heat until hot. Add onions; sauté until tender. Add water and bouillon granules; bring to a boil. Remove from heat. Add couscous and soy sauce; cover and let stand 5 minutes. Stir in tomato, parsley, and pepper. Yield: 4 (½-cup) servings.

PER SERVING: 92 CALORIES (9% FROM FAT)
FAT 1.0G (SATURATED FAT 0.1G)
PROTEIN 3.3G   CARBOHYDRATE 17.8G
CHOLESTEROL 0MG   SODIUM 302MG

GINGERED BROCCOLI

If you prefer fresh broccoli, cut it into flowerets and stir-fry until crisp-tender.

Vegetable cooking spray
1 teaspoon peanut oil
2 (⅛-inch) slices peeled gingerroot
1 large clove garlic, halved
8 frozen broccoli spears (about 6 ounces), thawed
1 teaspoon white wine vinegar
Dash of salt
Dash of pepper
Lemon rind curls (optional)
Orange rind curls (optional)

Coat a wok or large nonstick skillet with cooking spray; add oil. Heat at medium-high (375°) until hot. Add gingerroot; stir-fry 1 minute. Add garlic; stir-fry 1 minute. Discard gingerroot and garlic, reserving oil.

Add broccoli spears, vinegar, salt, and pepper to wok; stir-fry 1 to 2 minutes or until crisp-tender. If desired, garnish with lemon and orange curls. Yield: 4 (½-cup) servings.

PER SERVING: 23 CALORIES (57% FROM FAT)
FAT 1.4G (SATURATED FAT 0.2G)
PROTEIN 1.2G CARBOHYDRATE 2.1G
CHOLESTEROL 0MG SODIUM 46MG

FRESH BERRIES WITH LEMON CREAM

¼ cup plus 1 tablespoon sugar
2½ tablespoons cornstarch
1¼ cups skim milk
2 tablespoons frozen egg substitute, thawed
1 teaspoon grated lemon rind
2 tablespoons lemon juice
1 cup fresh raspberries, chilled
1 cup fresh blueberries, chilled
Fresh lemon balm sprigs (optional)

Combine sugar and cornstarch in a heavy saucepan; gradually add milk, stirring well. Cook over medium heat, stirring constantly, until thickened. Stir about one-fourth of hot mixture into egg substitute; add to remaining hot mixture, stirring constantly. Cook over medium-low heat 1 minute; remove from heat, and let cool slightly. Stir in lemon rind and lemon juice; cover and chill.

Combine berries, and divide evenly between individual dessert bowls. Spoon lemon cream evenly over fruit. Garnish with lemon balm sprigs, if desired. Yield: 4 servings.

PER SERVING: 147 CALORIES (2% FROM FAT)
FAT 0.4G (SATURATED FAT 0.1G)
PROTEIN 3.9G CARBOHYDRATE 33.4G
CHOLESTEROL 2MG SODIUM 54MG

Fresh Berries with Lemon Cream

FIRESIDE TRAY DINING

Let a cozy fireside be the setting for a special dinner. Prepare the greens for the salad early in the day, and assemble all the ingredients for the main dish and the vermicelli.

When guests arrive, heat the skillet to get dinner started. To round out the menu, offer commercial breadsticks with the main course. (Allow two breadsticks per serving for the correct calorie count.)

Dilled Scallops and Snow Peas

Vermicelli with Pimiento

Spinach-Radicchio Salad

Commercial breadsticks

Hot Spiced Wine

Serves 4
TOTAL CALORIES PER SERVING: 512
(CALORIES FROM FAT: 27%)

DILLED SCALLOPS AND SNOW PEAS

1 pound fresh sea scallops
Vegetable cooking spray
1 tablespoon margarine
½ pound fresh snow pea pods, trimmed
2 stalks celery, diagonally sliced
2 tablespoons dry white wine
1 tablespoon plus 1½ teaspoons lemon juice
¾ teaspoon dried dillweed or 2 teaspoons
   chopped fresh dill
¼ teaspoon freshly ground pepper
1 tablespoon chopped fresh parsley

Rinse scallops in cold water; drain and set scallops aside.

Coat a large nonstick skillet with cooking spray; add margarine, and place over medium-high heat until margarine melts. Add snow peas and celery; stir-fry 1 minute or until crisp-tender. Remove vegetables from skillet, using a slotted spoon; set vegetables aside.

Add scallops, wine, lemon juice, dillweed, and pepper to skillet. Bring mixture to a boil. Cover, reduce heat, and simmer 5 to 6 minutes or until scallops are opaque. Add reserved vegetables, and cook just until thoroughly heated. Sprinkle with chopped parsley, and serve with a slotted spoon. Yield: 4 servings.

PER SERVING: 157 CALORIES (23% FROM FAT)
FAT 4.0G (SATURATED FAT 0.7G)
PROTEIN 20.9G   CARBOHYDRATE 8.6G
CHOLESTEROL 37MG   SODIUM 237MG

Dilled Scallops and Snow Peas, Vermicelli with Pimiento, Spinach-Radicchio Salad, and Hot Spiced Wine

VERMICELLI WITH PIMIENTO

1 (4-ounce) jar sliced pimiento, undrained
Vegetable cooking spray
½ cup chopped onion
1 clove garlic, minced
4 ounces vermicelli, uncooked
1 tablespoon chopped fresh basil
2 tablespoons grated Parmesan cheese
1 teaspoon olive oil

Drain pimiento, reserving 1 teaspoon juice; set pimiento and juice aside.

Coat a nonstick skillet with cooking spray; place over medium heat until hot. Add chopped onion and garlic, and cook, stirring constantly, until tender; set aside.

Cook pasta according to package directions, omitting salt and fat. Drain well. Place in a warm serving bowl, and add pimiento, reserved 1 teaspoon pimiento juice, onion mixture, basil, and remaining ingredients. Toss well to coat before serving. Yield: 4 servings.

PER SERVING: 145 CALORIES (16% FROM FAT)
FAT 2.6G (SATURATED FAT 0.7G)
PROTEIN 5.3G   CARBOHYDRATE 25.0G
CHOLESTEROL 2MG   SODIUM 54MG

SPINACH-RADICCHIO SALAD

½ pound fresh spinach, washed and torn
¼ pound radicchio, washed
½ cup thinly sliced fresh mushrooms
1 sweet red pepper, seeded and thinly sliced
8 pitted ripe olives, sliced
¼ cup red wine vinegar
2 tablespoons lemon juice
1½ tablespoons olive oil
¼ teaspoon freshly ground pepper
1 tablespoon plus 1 teaspoon grated Parmesan cheese

Combine spinach, radicchio, mushrooms, red pepper, and olives in a large bowl. Cover and chill.

Combine vinegar, lemon juice, olive oil, and ground pepper in a jar; cover tightly, and shake vigorously. Pour vinegar mixture over spinach mixture, and toss; divide among 4 individual salad bowls. Sprinkle each salad with 1 teaspoon Parmesan cheese. Yield: 4 servings.

PER SERVING: 92 CALORIES (67% FROM FAT)
FAT 6.8G (SATURATED FAT 1.2G)
PROTEIN 3.2G   CARBOHYDRATE 6.5G
CHOLESTEROL 1MG   SODIUM 153MG

HOT SPICED WINE

4 whole cloves
1 (3-inch) stick cinnamon
1 cup unsweetened orange juice
½ cup water
3 thin slices lemon
3 thin slices orange
2½ cups dry red wine
4 (3-inch) sticks cinnamon (optional)

Tie cloves and 1 cinnamon stick in a cheesecloth bag; place in a large nonaluminum saucepan. Add orange juice and water; bring to a boil. Reduce heat, and simmer, uncovered, 10 minutes. Remove from heat; add lemon and orange slices. Cover and let stand 15 minutes.

Add wine to saucepan; bring to a simmer (do not boil). Strain into mugs, discarding spices and fruit slices. Garnish with additional cinnamon sticks, if desired. Serve warm. Yield: 4 (1-cup) servings.

PER SERVING: 36 CALORIES (0% FROM FAT)
FAT 0.0G (SATURATED FAT 0.0G)
PROTEIN 0.7G   CARBOHYDRATE 8.7G
CHOLESTEROL 0MG   SODIUM 12MG

VEGETARIAN CUISINE

This tropical vegetarian menu will appeal to even your most health-conscious guests. Stir-fry the garlic and vegetables for Caribbean Rice and Beans while you broil the simple tomato side dish. Don't forget the refreshing beverage, and top the meal off with a rum-flavored dessert. (The menu analysis includes one commercial dinner roll each.)

Caribbean Rice and Beans

Mustard-Glazed Broiled Tomatoes

Commercial dinner rolls

Rum Raisin Ice Milk

Tropical Cooler

Serves 6
TOTAL CALORIES PER SERVING: 733
(CALORIES FROM FAT: 9%)

CARIBBEAN RICE AND BEANS

6 (¼-inch-thick) slices fresh or canned
   pineapple
Vegetable cooking spray
3 tablespoons brown sugar, divided
1 teaspoon lime juice
2 teaspoons olive oil
¾ cup chopped green pepper
2 cloves garlic, minced
2 (15-ounce) cans black beans, drained
1 (2-ounce) jar diced pimiento, drained
2 tablespoons white vinegar
2 teaspoons peeled, grated gingerroot
1 teaspoon hot sauce
3 cups cooked brown rice (cooked without salt
   or fat)
¼ cup minced fresh cilantro

Coat both sides of pineapple slices with cooking spray. Rub 2 tablespoons sugar evenly on both sides of pineapple slices. Place pineapple on rack of a broiler pan coated with cooking spray. Broil 5½ inches from heat (with electric oven door partially opened) 4 minutes. Turn pineapple; broil 2 additional minutes or until lightly browned.

Combine remaining 1 tablespoon brown sugar and lime juice. Brush sugar mixture over pineapple. Cut each slice into 3 pieces; set aside.

Coat a wok or large nonstick skillet with cooking spray; add oil. Heat at medium-high (375°) until hot. Add green pepper and garlic; stir-fry until pepper is tender. Stir in beans and next 4 ingredients; cook 2 minutes or until thoroughly heated, stirring frequently.

Add rice and cilantro, stirring well. Spoon rice mixture evenly onto individual serving plates. Arrange pineapple pieces around rice mixture. Yield: 6 servings.

PER SERVING: 315 CALORIES (12% FROM FAT)
FAT 4.1G (SATURATED FAT 0.6G)
PROTEIN 10.8G CARBOHYDRATE 62.1G
CHOLESTEROL 0MG SODIUM 248MG

Caribbean Rice and Beans and Mustard-Glazed Broiled Tomato

MUSTARD-GLAZED BROILED TOMATOES

3 medium tomatoes (about 1 pound)
Vegetable cooking spray
2½ tablespoons coarse-grained mustard
2½ teaspoons brown sugar
1½ teaspoons minced fresh parsley

Cut tomatoes in half crosswise. Place tomato halves, cut side up, on rack of a broiler pan coated with cooking spray.

Combine mustard and brown sugar; stir well. Spread mustard mixture over cut sides of tomato. Broil 5½ inches from heat (with electric oven door partially open) 4 minutes or until lightly browned and bubbly. Sprinkle with parsley. Yield: 6 servings.

PER SERVING: 34 CALORIES (19% FROM FAT)
FAT 0.7G (SATURATED FAT 0.1G)
PROTEIN 0.9G   CARBOHYDRATE 6.9G
CHOLESTEROL 0MG   SODIUM 92MG

RUM RAISIN ICE MILK

⅓ cup raisins
⅓ cup dark rum
2 eggs
1 cup sugar
1 teaspoon cornstarch
2 cups skim milk
2 cups evaporated skimmed milk
½ teaspoon vanilla extract

Combine raisins and rum in a small saucepan; bring to a boil. Remove from heat; cover and let stand at room temperature 1 hour. Drain raisins; discard rum. Finely chop raisins, and set aside.

Beat eggs in a medium bowl at high speed of an electric mixer 3 minutes or until thick and pale. Combine sugar and cornstarch; gradually add to beaten eggs, beating constantly.

Transfer mixture to a large saucepan; stir in skim milk. Cook over medium heat, stirring constantly, until mixture thickens and just begins to boil. Remove from heat; cool. Stir in evaporated skimmed milk, vanilla, and raisins. Cover and chill.

Pour mixture into freezer container of a 1-gallon hand-turned or electric freezer. Freeze according to manufacturer's instructions. Pack freezer with additional ice and rock salt, and let stand 1 hour before serving. Yield: 11 (½-cup) servings.

PER SERVING: 153 CALORIES (6% FROM FAT)
FAT 1.1G (SATURATED FAT 0.4G)
PROTEIN 6.4G   CARBOHYDRATE 29.8G
CHOLESTEROL 43MG   SODIUM 90MG

TROPICAL COOLER

4¼ cups pineapple-orange juice, chilled
¼ cup plus 2 tablespoons frozen lemonade
    concentrate, thawed and undiluted
1½ cups ginger ale, chilled
Lemon slices (optional)
Fresh mint sprigs (optional)

Combine pineapple-orange juice and lemonade concentrate in a large pitcher; gently stir in ginger ale just before serving.

If desired, garnish with lemon slices and mint sprigs. Yield: 6 (1-cup) servings.

PER SERVING: 148 CALORIES (1% FROM FAT)
FAT 0.2G (SATURATED FAT 0.0G)
PROTEIN 0.4G   CARBOHYDRATE 37.8G
CHOLESTEROL 0MG   SODIUM 4MG

Tropical Cooler

Noodle Nests with Shrimp and Pork (recipe on page 52)

FISH & SHELLFISH ENTRÉES

*T*he secret to a successful fish stir-fry is to choose a firm-textured fish, such as salmon or swordfish, and to cook just until it can be flaked with a fork.

It is best to stir-fry fish and vegetables separately, and then combine these with the sauce just before serving. (The fish will be less likely to fall apart.)

If you prefer shellfish, shrimp and scallops are well suited to stir-frying. Both can be cooked quickly, and they hold up well during the constant tossing as they cook. And, like most mild shellfish, they are enhanced by the intense flavors associated with stir-fry cookery. Try Ginger-Scented Scallops and Vegetables (page 41) or Spicy Walnut Shrimp (page 49) for a taste treat.

CATFISH ORIENTAL

1 pound farm-raised catfish fillets
Vegetable cooking spray
1 tablespoon vegetable oil, divided
½ pound fresh snow pea pods, trimmed
1 cup sliced fresh mushrooms
¾ cup sliced green onions
¾ cup shredded carrot
½ cup canned, sliced water chestnuts
1 medium-size sweet red pepper, seeded and
    cut into strips
2 tablespoons low-sodium soy sauce
2 tablespoons lemon juice
2 teaspoons brown sugar
½ teaspoon ground ginger
3 cups cooked rice (cooked without salt or fat)
2 tablespoons sesame seeds

Rinse fillets with cold water, and pat dry. Cut into 2- x ¾-inch strips. Set aside.

Coat a wok or large nonstick skillet with cooking spray; add 1 teaspoon oil. Heat at medium-high (375°) for 2 minutes. Add snow peas and next 5 ingredients; stir-fry 3 minutes. Remove vegetables from wok, and set aside.

Add remaining 2 teaspoons oil to wok; heat at medium-high 2 minutes. Add fish; stir-fry 2 minutes or until fish flakes easily when tested with a fork. Reduce heat to low (200°). Add vegetables to wok. Combine soy sauce, lemon juice, sugar, and ginger. Pour over fish and vegetables; cook 2 minutes. Serve over rice, and sprinkle with sesame seeds. Yield: 4 servings.

PER SERVING: 431 CALORIES (23% FROM FAT)
FAT 11.2G (SATURATED FAT 2.1G)
PROTEIN 27.6G   CARBOHYDRATE 54.0G
CHOLESTEROL 66MG   SODIUM 331MG

SEAFOOD TACOS WITH CILANTRO SAUCE

1 tablespoon margarine
1 tablespoon all-purpose flour
1 cup skim milk
¼ cup plus 2 tablespoons (1½ ounces)
    shredded Monterey Jack cheese with
    jalapeño peppers
1 tablespoon minced fresh cilantro
½ pound flounder or sole fillets
1 tablespoon lime juice
¼ teaspoon ground red pepper
Vegetable cooking spray
¼ pound frozen tiny shrimp, thawed
¼ cup canned black beans, rinsed and drained
¼ cup finely chopped green onions
1 tablespoon minced fresh cilantro
1 tablespoon chopped sweet red pepper
1 tablespoon chopped sweet yellow pepper
4 (6-inch) flour tortillas

Melt margarine in a small, heavy saucepan over low heat; add flour, stirring until smooth. Cook 1 minute, stirring constantly. Gradually add milk; cook over medium heat, stirring constantly, until mixture is thickened and bubbly. Stir in cheese and 1 tablespoon cilantro; cook until cheese melts, stirring constantly. Set aside, and keep warm.

Sprinkle fillets with lime juice and ground red pepper. Cover and marinate in refrigerator 15 minutes.

Coat a large nonstick skillet with cooking spray; place over medium-high heat until hot. Add shrimp, and stir-fry until done. Set aside.

Coat skillet with cooking spray, and place over medium-high heat until hot. Add fillets, and cook until fish flakes easily with a fork. Cut into strips.

Combine reserved cheese mixture, shrimp, beans, and next 4 ingredients in a large bowl; set aside. Heat tortillas according to package directions. Spoon shrimp mixture evenly over half of each tortilla. Top with fish strips, and fold tortillas in half. Serve immediately. Yield: 4 servings.

PER SERVING: 310 CALORIES (30% FROM FAT)
FAT 10.3G (SATURATED FAT 3.3G)
PROTEIN 25.5G   CARBOHYDRATE 27.8G
CHOLESTEROL 80MG   SODIUM 409MG

THAI SALMON AND SPINACH

½ cup canned no-salt-added chicken broth, undiluted
1 tablespoon lime juice
1 tablespoon low-sodium soy sauce
2 teaspoons cornstarch
2 teaspoons brown sugar
¼ teaspoon dried crushed red pepper
Vegetable cooking spray
1 pound skinned salmon fillet, cut into 1-inch pieces
1 (10-ounce) package washed and trimmed fresh spinach
1 cup julienne-sliced sweet red pepper
1 cup fresh bean sprouts
½ teaspoon grated lime rind
½ teaspoon coconut extract
4 cups cooked rice (cooked without salt or fat)

Combine first 6 ingredients in a small bowl; stir well, and set aside.

Coat a wok or large nonstick skillet with cooking spray, and heat at high (400°) until hot. Add fish; stir-fry 3 minutes or until fish flakes easily when tested with a fork. Remove fish from wok; set aside, and keep warm.

Reduce heat to medium-high (375°), and add half of spinach to wok; stir-fry 30 seconds. Add remaining spinach, and stir-fry 30 seconds. Add sweet red pepper and bean sprouts; stir-fry 1 minute. Add broth mixture; cook 1 minute, stirring constantly. Return fish to wok; stir well. Reduce heat, and stir in lime rind and coconut extract. Serve immediately over rice. Yield: 4 servings.

PER SERVING: 437 CALORIES (16% FROM FAT)
FAT 7.6G (SATURATED FAT 1.3G)
PROTEIN 31.8G CARBOHYDRATE 58.5G
CHOLESTEROL 44MG SODIUM 207MG

RED SNAPPER COUSCOUS

Couscous can be found among rice and other grains in your supermarket.

2 teaspoons olive oil
½ cup chopped onion
½ cup julienne-sliced sweet red pepper
1 clove garlic, minced
¼ teaspoon salt
¼ teaspoon ground cumin
¼ teaspoon ground cinnamon
¼ teaspoon paprika
⅛ teaspoon ground red pepper
1 cup cubed red potato
1 cup canned vegetable broth, undiluted
1 tablespoon tomato paste
1 cup frozen artichoke hearts
½ pound red snapper fillet, cut into bite-size pieces
4 cups cooked couscous (cooked without salt or fat)
1 tablespoon chopped fresh cilantro

Heat oil in a wok or large nonstick skillet at medium-high (375°) until hot. Add onion, sweet red pepper, and garlic; stir-fry 3 minutes. Add salt, cumin, cinnamon, paprika, and pepper; stir-fry 30 seconds. Add potato, broth, and tomato paste to wok; bring to a boil. Cover, reduce heat, and simmer 10 minutes.

Add artichoke hearts and fish to potato mixture; cover and cook 10 minutes or until fish flakes easily when tested with a fork, stirring occasionally.

For each serving, spoon 1 cup fish mixture over 1 cup couscous, and sprinkle with chopped cilantro. Yield: 4 servings.

PER SERVING: 360 CALORIES (12% FROM FAT)
FAT 4.6G (SATURATED FAT 0.6G)
PROTEIN 25.1G CARBOHYDRATE 56.4G
CHOLESTEROL 27MG SODIUM 399MG

Island Fish Fajitas

ISLAND FISH FAJITAS

2 tablespoons fresh lime juice
½ teaspoon lemon-pepper seasoning
¼ teaspoon ground cumin
1½ pounds snapper fillets, skinned
4 (10-inch) flour tortillas
Vegetable cooking spray
1 teaspoon vegetable oil
1 cup vertically sliced purple onion
½ cup sweet red pepper strips
½ cup green pepper strips
Pineapple Salsa

Combine lime juice, lemon-pepper seasoning, and cumin in a heavy-duty, zip-top plastic bag; add fillets. Seal bag, and shake well to coat. Marinate fish in refrigerator 20 minutes.

Heat tortillas according to package directions.

Coat a large nonstick skillet with cooking spray. Add oil, and place over medium-high heat until hot. Add sliced onion and peppers, and stir-fry 5 minutes or until crisp-tender. Remove from skillet; set aside, and keep warm.

Place fillets in skillet; cook over medium-high heat 3 minutes on each side or until fish flakes easily when tested with a fork. Remove from heat, and cut into ½-inch-wide strips. Divide fish and pepper mixture among tortillas, and roll up. Spoon salsa evenly over fajitas. Yield: 4 servings.

PINEAPPLE SALSA
1 cup finely chopped fresh pineapple
¼ cup minced purple onion
1 tablespoon minced seeded jalapeño pepper

Combine all ingredients in a small bowl, and stir well. Cover and chill. Yield: 4 (¼-cup) servings.

PER SERVING: 417 CALORIES (18% FROM FAT)
FAT 8.2G (SATURATED FAT 1.4G)
PROTEIN 40.9G   CARBOHYDRATE 43.3G
CHOLESTEROL 63MG   SODIUM 392MG

SWORDFISH STIR-FRY

2 (8-ounce) swordfish steaks (1 inch thick)
2 tablespoons low-sodium soy sauce
2 tablespoons dry sherry
1 teaspoon minced garlic
1 teaspoon peeled, minced gingerroot
½ cup canned low-sodium chicken broth,
    undiluted
¼ cup unsweetened pineapple juice
1 tablespoon cornstarch
3 tablespoons no-salt-added tomato paste
2 tablespoons vinegar
1 teaspoon sugar
Vegetable cooking spray
1 tablespoon peanut oil
1 small onion, thinly sliced
⅔ cup diagonally sliced carrot
¼ pound fresh snow pea pods, trimmed
1⅓ cups sliced fresh mushrooms
⅓ cup chopped green onions
1 cup fresh broccoli flowerets
3 cups cooked rice (cooked without salt or fat)

Cut swordfish into 1-inch pieces; place in a shallow dish. Combine soy sauce, sherry, garlic, and gingerroot, stirring well; pour over fish. Cover and marinate in refrigerator up to 4 hours.

Combine chicken broth and next 5 ingredients; stir well. Set aside.

Remove fish from marinade, discarding marinade. Coat a wok or large nonstick skillet with cooking spray. Add oil, and heat at medium-high (375°) until hot. Add fish, and stir-fry 3 minutes or until tender. Remove from wok; set aside, and keep warm.

Coat wok with cooking spray; heat at medium-high until hot. Add onion, and stir-fry 1 minute. Add carrot, and stir-fry 1 minute. Add snow peas, mushrooms, and green onions; stir-fry 2 minutes or until crisp-tender. Add broccoli, and stir-fry 1 minute. Return fish to wok. Stir in reserved broth mixture. Cook, stirring constantly, until mixture is thickened; serve over rice. Yield: 6 servings.

PER SERVING: 304 CALORIES (18% FROM FAT)
FAT 6.2G (SATURATED FAT 1.4G)
PROTEIN 21.3G   CARBOHYDRATE 39.8G
CHOLESTEROL 32MG   SODIUM 250MG

SWORDFISH OVER NOODLES

If you can't find cellophane noodles, substitute a package of low-fat ramen noodles, minus the seasoning packet. Shrimp or chicken can replace the swordfish.

1 (4-ounce) package cellophane noodles
½ cup canned no-salt-added chicken broth,
    undiluted
1 tablespoon sugar
1 tablespoon cornstarch
3 tablespoons fresh lime juice
1 tablespoon fish sauce
1 teaspoon chili puree with garlic
Vegetable cooking spray
1 (8-ounce) swordfish fillet, cut into 1-inch
    pieces
1 teaspoon vegetable oil
½ sweet red pepper, thinly sliced
2 cloves garlic, crushed
1 tablespoon peeled, minced gingerroot
1 large cucumber, peeled, seeded, and sliced
⅓ cup chopped green onions
¼ cup chopped fresh cilantro

Cook cellophane noodles according to package directions; drain noodles, and set aside.

Combine broth and next 5 ingredients, stirring well; set aside.

Coat a wok or large nonstick skillet with cooking spray; heat at medium-high (375°) until hot. Add fish to wok, and stir-fry 3 minutes or until tender. Remove fish from wok; set aside, and keep warm.

Add oil to wok; add sweet red pepper, garlic, and gingerroot, and stir-fry 1 minute. Add cucumber, and stir-fry 30 seconds.

Add broth mixture to wok, stirring well; bring to a boil. Boil 1 minute. Return fish to wok, and cook just until thoroughly heated. Stir in green onions and cilantro. Serve over cellophane noodles. Yield: 2 servings.

PER SERVING: 457 CALORIES (17% FROM FAT)
FAT 8.7G (SATURATED FAT 1.6G)
PROTEIN 24.8G   CARBOHYDRATE 69.0G
CHOLESTEROL 44MG   SODIUM 757MG

OYSTERS AND PASTA SHELLS

If fresh oregano is not available, use about ³/₄ teaspoon dried oregano instead.

Butter-flavored vegetable cooking spray
1 tablespoon reduced-calorie margarine
1½ cups chopped fresh mushrooms
¼ cup chopped green onions
1 (10-ounce) container fresh oysters, drained
½ cup canned low-sodium chicken broth, undiluted
2 tablespoons dry white wine
2 teaspoons chopped fresh oregano
¼ teaspoon hot sauce
¼ cup chopped fresh parsley
1 tablespoon fresh lemon juice
8 ounces small pasta shells, uncooked
²/₃ cup freshly grated Parmesan cheese

Coat a large nonstick skillet with cooking spray; add margarine. Place over medium-high heat until margarine melts. Add mushrooms and green onions; stir-fry 1 minute. Add oysters, and stir-fry 2 minutes. Add broth and next 3 ingredients; cook 2 minutes. Add parsley and lemon juice; stir well. Remove from heat, and keep warm.

Cook pasta according to package directions, omitting salt and fat; drain. Place pasta in a serving bowl, and add oyster mixture; toss gently. Sprinkle with cheese. Serve immediately. Yield: 5 (1-cup) servings.

PER SERVING: 284 CALORIES (24% FROM FAT)
FAT 7.6G (SATURATED FAT 2.9G)
PROTEIN 15.1G   CARBOHYDRATE 37.4G
CHOLESTEROL 35MG   SODIUM 324MG

SCALLOP-VEGETABLE STIR-FRY

Try serving this stir-fry with cellophane noodles instead of rice. After cooking, the brittle, wire-thin strands become translucent.

¾ cup canned no-salt-added chicken broth, undiluted
1 tablespoon cornstarch
1½ tablespoons low-sodium soy sauce
½ teaspoon light-colored sesame oil
Vegetable cooking spray
2 teaspoons vegetable oil
1¼ cups diagonally sliced carrot
1 cup sliced fresh mushrooms
1 (6-ounce) package frozen snow pea pods, thawed
½ cup diagonally sliced green onions
1 tablespoon peeled, minced gingerroot
½ pound fresh bay scallops
Cooked cellophane noodles (optional)

Combine first 4 ingredients in a small bowl, stirring well; set aside.

Coat a wok or large nonstick skillet with cooking spray; add vegetable oil, and heat at medium-high (375°) until hot. Add carrot; stir-fry 1 minute. Add mushrooms; stir-fry 1 minute. Add snow peas, and stir-fry 1 minute. Remove vegetables from wok; set aside, and keep warm. Wipe drippings from wok with a paper towel.

Coat wok with cooking spray. Add green onions and gingerroot; stir-fry 30 seconds. Add scallops; stir-fry 1 to 2 minutes or until scallops are opaque. Add reserved vegetables to wok; stir well. Pour reserved broth mixture over vegetable mixture. Cook, stirring constantly, 1 minute or until slightly thickened and thoroughly heated. Transfer to a serving platter. Serve with cooked cellophane noodles, if desired. Yield: 2 servings.

PER SERVING: 267 CALORIES (26% FROM FAT)
FAT 7.6G (SATURATED FAT 1.2G)
PROTEIN 23.9G   CARBOHYDRATE 23.9G
CHOLESTEROL 37MG   SODIUM 510MG

Scallop-Vegetable Stir-Fry

CURRIED SCALLOPS AND VEGETABLES

Vegetable cooking spray
1½ cups shredded carrot
1 cup diced celery
¼ teaspoon pepper
2 teaspoons reduced-calorie margarine
1 pound fresh bay scallops
1 tablespoon dry white wine
½ teaspoon curry powder
¼ teaspoon salt
Chopped fresh chives (optional)

Coat a large nonstick skillet with cooking spray; place over medium-high heat until hot. Add carrot, celery, and pepper; stir-fry until vegetables are crisp-tender. Set mixture aside, and keep warm.

Coat skillet with cooking spray; add margarine. Place over medium-high heat until margarine melts. Add scallops; stir-fry 1 minute. Add white wine, curry powder, and salt; cook, stirring frequently, 4 to 5 additional minutes or until scallops are opaque.

Spoon carrot mixture evenly onto 4 individual serving plates; top evenly with scallop mixture. Garnish with chopped fresh chives, if desired. Yield: 4 servings.

PER SERVING: 133 CALORIES (17% FROM FAT)
FAT 2.5G (SATURATED FAT 0.3G)
PROTEIN 19.6G CARBOHYDRATE 7.4G
CHOLESTEROL 37MG SODIUM 387MG

Buying Scallops

When shopping for scallops, you'll find two types: bay scallops, which are only about ½ inch in diameter, and sea scallops, which average 1½ inches in diameter. These shellfish should have a sweet smell and a moist sheen, and they should be cooked or frozen within a day or two of purchase. Count on 1 pound yielding four servings.

STIR-FRIED SCALLOPS AND VEGETABLES

½ cup water
1 tablespoon cornstarch
2 tablespoons dry sherry
2 tablespoons low-sodium teriyaki marinade and sauce
½ teaspoon chicken-flavored bouillon granules
½ teaspoon ground cumin
½ teaspoon ground ginger
4 ounces fresh snow pea pods, trimmed
Vegetable cooking spray
1 teaspoon vegetable oil
¾ cup fresh corn cut from cob (about 2 ears)
6 green onions, cut into 1½-inch pieces
1 tablespoon minced garlic
1 pound sea scallops, cut in half
3 tablespoons chopped walnuts, toasted

Combine first 7 ingredients in a small bowl; stir well. Set aside.

Cut snow peas lengthwise into julienne strips, and set aside.

Coat a wok or large nonstick skillet with cooking spray; add oil, and heat at medium (350°) until hot. Add corn; cook 2 minutes, stirring constantly. Increase heat to medium-high (375°). Add snow peas, green onions, and garlic; stir-fry 3 minutes. Remove vegetables from wok; set aside. Wipe wok dry with a paper towel.

Coat wok with cooking spray; heat at medium-high until hot. Add scallops, and stir-fry 3 minutes or until scallops are opaque. Remove from wok, and set aside.

Add reserved teriyaki mixture to wok; cook, stirring constantly, 1 minute or until mixture is thickened. Return vegetables and scallops to wok. Cook, stirring constantly, until mixture is thoroughly heated. Transfer to a serving platter, and sprinkle with walnuts. Serve immediately. Yield: 4 servings.

PER SERVING: 213 CALORIES (27% FROM FAT)
FAT 6.3G (SATURATED FAT 0.6G)
PROTEIN 23.1G CARBOHYDRATE 16.7G
CHOLESTEROL 37MG SODIUM 445MG

Scallop-Artichoke Stir-Fry

SCALLOP-ARTICHOKE STIR-FRY

Vegetable cooking spray
1 (14-ounce) can artichoke hearts, drained and
    quartered
2 cups sliced fresh mushrooms
½ cup julienne-sliced green pepper
½ cup julienne-sliced sweet red pepper
2 cloves garlic, minced
1 teaspoon vegetable oil
1 pound fresh sea scallops
1 tablespoon cornstarch
1 teaspoon sugar
¼ teaspoon chicken-flavored bouillon granules
⅛ teaspoon pepper
¾ cup water
2 tablespoons lime juice
2 cups cooked brown rice (cooked without salt
    or fat)

Coat a wok or large nonstick skillet with cooking spray; heat at high (400°) until hot. Add artichokes and next 4 ingredients; stir-fry 5 minutes. Remove vegetables from wok; set aside. Add oil, and heat until hot. Add half of scallops; stir-fry 2 minutes or until scallops are opaque. Remove scallops from wok; repeat with remaining scallops. Set scallops aside.

Combine cornstarch and next 5 ingredients in a small bowl, stirring well; add to wok. Cook 1 minute or until thickened and bubbly. Return vegetables and scallops to wok, and cook just until thoroughly heated. For each serving, spoon 1 cup scallop mixture over ½ cup rice. Yield: 4 servings.

PER SERVING: 290 CALORIES (11% FROM FAT)
FAT 3.5G (SATURATED FAT 0.6G)
PROTEIN 25.0G   CARBOHYDRATE 40.7G
CHOLESTEROL 37MG   SODIUM 453MG

SCALLOPS PROVENÇAL

2 teaspoons olive oil
1 pound fresh sea scallops
½ cup thinly sliced onion, separated into rings
1 clove garlic, minced
1 cup diced, unpeeled plum tomato
¼ cup chopped ripe olives
1 tablespoon dried basil
¼ teaspoon dried thyme
⅛ teaspoon salt
⅛ teaspoon freshly ground pepper

Heat oil in a wok or large nonstick skillet at medium-high (375°) until hot. Add scallops; stir-fry 4 minutes or until opaque. Remove scallops from wok with a slotted spoon. Set aside; keep warm.

Add onion and garlic to wok; stir-fry 1 minute. Add tomato and remaining 5 ingredients; stir-fry 2 minutes. Spoon sauce over scallops. Yield: 4 servings.

PER SERVING: 150 CALORIES (25% FROM FAT)
FAT 4.2G (SATURATED FAT 0.6G)
PROTEIN 19.9G   CARBOHYDRATE 8.0G
CHOLESTEROL 37MG   SODIUM 332MG

SWEET-AND-HOT SCALLOPS

Vegetable cooking spray
2 teaspoons peanut oil
½ cup diagonally sliced carrot
½ cup sliced onion
1 (8-ounce) can pineapple chunks in juice, undrained
6 ounces fresh snow pea pods, trimmed
1 (8-ounce) can water chestnuts, drained
1 pound fresh sea scallops
¼ cup chopped green onions
½ cup canned low-sodium chicken broth, undiluted
1 tablespoon cornstarch
2 tablespoons rice wine vinegar
1 tablespoon hot bean paste
1 teaspoon low-sodium soy sauce
3 cups cooked rice (cooked without salt or fat)

Coat a wok or large nonstick skillet with cooking spray; add peanut oil, and heat at medium-high (375°) until hot. Add carrot, and stir-fry 1 minute. Add onion, and stir-fry 1 minute.

Drain pineapple, reserving ¼ cup juice. Add pineapple, snow peas, and water chestnuts to mixture in wok; stir-fry 1 minute. Add scallops and green onions; stir-fry 3 minutes. Combine reserved juice, broth, and next 4 ingredients; add to scallop mixture. Cook, stirring constantly, until thickened and thoroughly heated. Serve over rice. Yield: 6 servings.

PER SERVING: 275 CALORIES (9% FROM FAT)
FAT 2.8G (SATURATED FAT 0.4G)
PROTEIN 17.0G   CARBOHYDRATE 44.2G
CHOLESTEROL 25MG   SODIUM 177MG

SCALLOPS WITH FRESH PINEAPPLE

1 teaspoon dark sesame oil
1 pound fresh sea scallops
2 teaspoons low-sodium soy sauce
⅛ teaspoon dried crushed red pepper
1 clove garlic, minced
1 cup cubed fresh pineapple
⅓ cup chopped fresh basil
1 teaspoon peeled, grated gingerroot
1 tablespoon water
1 teaspoon cornstarch
2 cups cooked rice (cooked without salt or fat)
Fresh basil sprigs (optional)

Heat oil in a wok or large nonstick skillet at medium-high (375°) until hot. Add scallops and next 3 ingredients; stir-fry 4 minutes or until opaque. Add pineapple, chopped basil, and gingerroot; stir well.

Combine water and cornstarch; stir well. Add to scallop mixture. Bring to a boil; cook, stirring constantly, 1 minute or until thickened. For each serving, spoon ½ cup scallop mixture over ½ cup rice. Garnish with basil sprigs, if desired. Yield: 4 servings.

PER SERVING: 243 CALORIES (9% FROM FAT)
FAT 2.3G (SATURATED FAT 0.3G)
PROTEIN 21.3G   CARBOHYDRATE 32.6G
CHOLESTEROL 37MG   SODIUM 249MG

Scallops with Fresh Pineapple

Ginger-Scented Scallops and Vegetables

GINGER-SCENTED SCALLOPS AND VEGETABLES

1 tablespoon vegetable oil, divided
2 teaspoons peeled, minced gingerroot
1 clove garlic, minced
1½ cups fresh snow pea pods (about ¼ pound), trimmed
1 cup thinly sliced carrot
1 tablespoon low-sodium soy sauce
2 teaspoons cornstarch
⅛ teaspoon salt
1 pound fresh sea scallops
¼ cup diagonally sliced green onions
3 cups cooked rice (cooked without salt or fat)

Heat 2 teaspoons oil in a wok or large nonstick skillet at medium-high (375°) until hot. Add gingerroot and garlic, and stir-fry 30 seconds. Add snow peas and carrot; stir-fry 1 minute. Remove vegetables from wok; set aside, and keep warm.

Combine soy sauce, cornstarch, and salt, stirring well; set aside. Reduce heat to medium (350°). Add remaining 1 teaspoon oil and scallops to wok; stir-fry 3 minutes or until scallops are opaque. Return vegetables to wok; add soy sauce mixture and green onions. Cook 1 minute, stirring constantly. For each serving, spoon ¾ cup scallop mixture over ¾ cup rice. Yield: 4 servings.

PER SERVING: 331 CALORIES (13% FROM FAT)
FAT 4.6G (SATURATED FAT 0.7G)
PROTEIN 23.5G CARBOHYDRATE 46.5G
CHOLESTEROL 37MG SODIUM 363MG

FYI

The freshest gingerroot has smooth skin; wrinkled skin means that the root is old and that the flesh will be dry. Wrapped tightly, gingerroot will keep for a week in the refrigerator or up to two months in the freezer.

LINGUINE WITH SCALLOP SAUCE

6 ounces linguine, uncooked
1 pound fresh sea scallops
Vegetable cooking spray
1 teaspoon olive oil
¾ cup chopped onion
1 clove garlic, minced
¼ teaspoon pepper
⅛ teaspoon salt
2½ cups seeded, chopped unpeeled plum tomato (about 1 pound)
⅓ cup dry white wine
¼ cup sliced ripe olives
1 tablespoon dried basil
2 tablespoons grated Parmesan cheese
2 tablespoons chopped fresh parsley

Cook linguine according to package directions, omitting salt and fat. Drain; set aside, and keep warm. Cut scallops in half crosswise; set aside.

Coat a wok or large nonstick skillet with cooking spray; add oil, and heat at medium-high (375°) until hot. Add onion and garlic, and stir-fry 2 minutes. Remove from wok; set aside.

Add scallops, pepper, and salt to wok; stir-fry 2 minutes or until scallops are opaque. Remove scallops from wok with a slotted spoon, and set aside.

Add tomato and next 3 ingredients to wok; cook at medium (350°) for 2 minutes. Return onion mixture and scallops to wok; cook 1 minute, stirring occasionally. Combine pasta and scallop mixture in a bowl; toss well. Sprinkle with cheese and parsley. Yield: 4 (1½-cup) servings.

PER SERVING: 330 CALORIES (13% FROM FAT)
FAT 4.9G (SATURATED FAT 1.0G)
PROTEIN 27.2G CARBOHYDRATE 44.2G
CHOLESTEROL 39MG SODIUM 386MG

STIR-FRY SHRIMP

1/3 cup fresh lime juice
1/3 cup dry sherry
3 tablespoons hoisin sauce
1 tablespoon chili puree with garlic
2 teaspoons dark sesame oil
1 tablespoon cornstarch
2 pounds unpeeled medium-size fresh shrimp
2 teaspoons vegetable oil
4 cloves garlic, minced
2 tablespoons peeled, minced gingerroot
3 carrots, scraped and thinly sliced
1 sweet red pepper, thinly sliced
1/2 pound fresh snow pea pods, trimmed
1/4 pound fresh bean sprouts
2 bunches green onions, sliced
3 cups cooked rice (cooked without salt or fat)

Combine first 6 ingredients in a small bowl, and set aside.

Peel and devein shrimp; set aside.

Heat vegetable oil in a wok or large nonstick skillet at high (400°) until hot. Add garlic and next 4 ingredients; stir-fry 3 minutes. Add shrimp and bean sprouts, and stir-fry 2 minutes or until shrimp turn pink.

Add green onions and lime juice mixture; bring to a boil. Boil 1 minute or until thickened. Serve immediately over rice. Yield: 4 servings.

PER SERVING: 472 CALORIES (15% FROM FAT)
FAT 7.5G (SATURATED FAT 1.1G)
PROTEIN 31.5G CARBOHYDRATE 64.7G
CHOLESTEROL 172MG SODIUM 540MG

SHRIMP AND SNOW PEAS

1/2 cup dry white wine
1 tablespoon low-sodium soy sauce
1 1/2 teaspoons cornstarch
1 teaspoon chopped fresh parsley
3/4 teaspoon dried basil
2 teaspoons lime juice
1/8 teaspoon garlic salt
1/8 teaspoon freshly ground pepper
1 pound unpeeled medium-size fresh shrimp
Vegetable cooking spray
1 teaspoon vegetable oil
6 green onions, chopped
1/4 pound fresh snow pea pods, trimmed
1 bay leaf
2 cups cooked rice (cooked without salt or fat)

Combine first 8 ingredients in a bowl; stir well, and set aside.

Peel and devein shrimp; set aside. Coat a wok or large nonstick skillet with cooking spray; add oil, and heat at medium-high (375°) until hot. Add green onions and snow peas; stir-fry 2 minutes or until crisp-tender. Remove from wok; set aside.

Add shrimp to wok; stir-fry 3 minutes or until shrimp turn pink.

Add wine mixture and bay leaf to wok; bring to a boil, and cook until thickened and bubbly, stirring occasionally. Add vegetables to wok, and cook until thoroughly heated.

Remove and discard bay leaf. Serve over rice. Yield: 4 servings.

PER SERVING: 237 CALORIES (11% FROM FAT)
FAT 3.0G (SATURATED FAT 0.5G)
PROTEIN 20.5G CARBOHYDRATE 30.2G
CHOLESTEROL 129MG SODIUM 293MG

Deveining Shrimp

When cooking small and medium shrimp, removing the vein is simply a matter of preference. In large and jumbo shrimp, however, the vein that runs along the back may contain grit, and so it is best to remove the vein.

Here's how: Using a sharp paring knife, slit the shrimp down the back. Then carefully pull away the vein using the tip of the knife.

Shrimp and Snow Peas

ORIENTAL SHRIMP STIR-FRY

1 pound fresh asparagus spears
2 tablespoons dry white wine
1 tablespoon white wine vinegar
1 tablespoon low-sodium soy sauce
2 pounds unpeeled medium-size fresh shrimp
Vegetable cooking spray
2 teaspoons vegetable oil
⅔ cup minced green onions
2 tablespoons peeled, minced gingerroot
1 teaspoon minced garlic
3 cups chopped Chinese cabbage
1 tablespoon cornstarch
1 tablespoon water

Snap off tough ends of asparagus. Remove scales from stalks with a knife or vegetable peeler, if desired. Cut asparagus diagonally into 1-inch pieces. Set aside.

Combine wine, vinegar, and soy sauce in a small bowl, stirring well; set aside.

Peel and devein shrimp; set aside.

Coat a wok or large nonstick skillet with cooking spray; add oil, and heat at medium-high (375°) until hot. Add green onions, gingerroot, and minced garlic; stir-fry 1 minute. Add shrimp and asparagus, and stir-fry 5 minutes. Add wine mixture and cabbage; stir-fry 5 minutes.

Combine cornstarch and water in a small bowl, stirring until smooth. Add to shrimp mixture. Cook, stirring constantly, until mixture is thickened. Yield: 6 servings.

PER SERVING: 164 CALORIES (21% FROM FAT)
FAT 3.8G (SATURATED FAT 0.7G)
PROTEIN 25.3G CARBOHYDRATE 6.6G
CHOLESTEROL 172MG SODIUM 248MG

SZECHUAN SHRIMP STIR-FRY

¼ cup canned no-salt-added chicken broth, undiluted
1 tablespoon low-sodium soy sauce
1 tablespoon tomato puree
2 teaspoons sugar
1 teaspoon cornstarch
1 teaspoon dried crushed red pepper
1½ pounds unpeeled medium-size fresh shrimp
Vegetable cooking spray
4 green onions, cut into 1-inch pieces
1 tablespoon peeled, minced gingerroot
4 cups cooked rice (cooked without salt or fat)

Combine first 6 ingredients in a small bowl, and set aside.

Peel and devein shrimp. Coat a wok or large nonstick skillet with cooking spray; heat at medium-high (375°) until hot. Add shrimp, green onions, and gingerroot; stir-fry 3 to 4 minutes or until shrimp turn pink. Add chicken broth mixture, and cook 1 minute or until sauce is slightly thickened and bubbly, stirring frequently. Spoon rice onto a serving platter; top with shrimp mixture. Yield: 4 servings.

PER SERVING: 328 CALORIES (5% FROM FAT)
FAT 1.9G (SATURATED FAT 0.3G)
PROTEIN 21.6G CARBOHYDRATE 53.2G
CHOLESTEROL 129MG SODIUM 243MG

Did You Know?

Chinese cuisine is divided into five categories that are based on geographic regions: Canton, Fukien, Hunan, Shantung, and Szechuan. Szechuan food tends to be particularly fiery, with much of its hot spiciness coming from gingerroot and dried red peppers.

SWEET-AND-SOUR SHRIMP IN FRUIT SAUCE

(pictured on page 2)

2 pounds unpeeled large fresh shrimp
1 tablespoon vegetable oil
¼ cup sugar
2 cups cubed fresh pineapple
2 cups cubed papaya
1⅓ cups unsweetened orange juice
1 teaspoon salt
2 teaspoons lime juice
¼ cup white wine vinegar
1 tablespoon plus 1 teaspoon cornstarch
⅓ cup chopped fresh cilantro
6 cups cooked rice (cooked without salt or fat)
Fresh cilantro sprigs (optional)

  Peel and devein shrimp; set aside. Heat oil in a wok or large nonstick skillet at medium-high (375°) until hot. Add shrimp; stir-fry 4 minutes or until shrimp turn pink. Remove from wok; set aside.
  Combine sugar and next 5 ingredients in wok. Combine vinegar and cornstarch, stirring well; add to wok. Bring to a boil; cook, stirring constantly, 1 minute or until thickened.
  Return shrimp to wok. Reduce heat to low (200°), and cook, stirring constantly, 1 minute or until thoroughly heated. Remove from heat; stir in chopped cilantro. For each serving, spoon 1 cup shrimp mixture over 1 cup rice. Garnish with cilantro sprigs, if desired. Yield: 6 servings.

PER SERVING: 479 CALORIES (9% FROM FAT)
FAT 4.9G (SATURATED FAT 0.8G)
PROTEIN 29.1G CARBOHYDRATE 77.9G
CHOLESTEROL 180MG SODIUM 571MG

APRICOT-GINGER SHRIMP STIR-FRY

1½ pounds unpeeled large fresh shrimp
Vegetable cooking spray
1 tablespoon sesame oil
1 cup diagonally sliced carrot
2 teaspoons peeled, minced gingerroot
1 clove garlic, minced
1 cup julienne-sliced green pepper
1 cup julienne-sliced sweet red pepper
1 (8-ounce) can pineapple tidbits in juice, undrained
¼ cup no-sugar-added apricot spread
1½ tablespoons low-sodium soy sauce
2 teaspoons cornstarch
½ teaspoon dried crushed red pepper
⅛ teaspoon salt
2½ cups cooked rice (cooked without salt or fat)

  Peel and devein shrimp; set aside.
  Coat a wok or large nonstick skillet with cooking spray; add oil, and heat at medium-high (375°) until hot. Add carrot, gingerroot, and minced garlic; stir-fry 2 minutes. Add sliced peppers, and stir-fry 2 minutes. Add shrimp, and stir-fry 3 to 4 minutes or until shrimp turn pink.
  Drain pineapple, reserving juice. Add pineapple to shrimp mixture; stir-fry 30 seconds.
  Combine reserved pineapple juice, apricot spread, and next 4 ingredients, stirring well. Add juice mixture to shrimp mixture; stir-fry 1 minute or until thickened. Serve immediately over rice. Yield: 5 servings.

PER SERVING: 334 CALORIES (14% FROM FAT)
FAT 5.0G (SATURATED FAT 0.8G)
PROTEIN 23.5G CARBOHYDRATE 47.0G
CHOLESTEROL 155MG SODIUM 335MG

Shrimp Stir-Fry with Ginger Sauce

SHRIMP STIR-FRY WITH GINGER SAUCE

1¼ pounds unpeeled medium-size fresh
    shrimp
Vegetable cooking spray
4 cups sliced yellow squash
1 cup sliced zucchini
⅔ cup chopped sweet red pepper
½ cup diagonally sliced celery
½ pound sliced fresh mushrooms
2 tablespoons cornstarch
1 tablespoon brown sugar
3 tablespoons low-sodium soy sauce
1 (10½-ounce) can low-sodium chicken broth
2 to 3 teaspoons peeled, grated gingerroot or ⅛
    to ½ teaspoon ground ginger
2 cloves garlic, minced
6 cups cooked rice (cooked without salt or fat)

Peel and devein shrimp. Coat a wok or large non-stick skillet with cooking spray; heat at medium-high (375°) until hot. Add shrimp; stir-fry 2 minutes or until shrimp turn pink. Remove from wok, and set aside.

Combine yellow squash, zucchini, sweet red pepper, celery, and mushrooms; add half of vegetables to wok. Stir-fry 3 minutes at medium-high. Remove from wok, and set aside. Repeat procedure with remaining vegetables; stir-fry 3 minutes, and set aside.

Combine cornstarch, brown sugar, soy sauce, and chicken broth, stirring well. Add gingerroot and garlic to wok; stir-fry 30 seconds. Add cornstarch mixture; bring to a boil, stirring constantly. Cook 1 minute or until thickened.

Stir in shrimp and vegetables; cook 1 minute. For each serving, spoon 1 cup shrimp mixture over 1 cup rice. Yield: 6 servings.

PER SERVING: 362 CALORIES (6% FROM FAT)
FAT 2.4G (SATURATED FAT 0.3G)
PROTEIN 22.6G   CARBOHYDRATE 61.7G
CHOLESTEROL 115MG   SODIUM 443MG

STIR-FRIED SHRIMP WITH LEEKS

1½ pounds unpeeled medium-size fresh
    shrimp
¾ cup canned low-sodium chicken broth,
    undiluted
1 tablespoon cornstarch
2 tablespoons dry sherry
2 tablespoons low-sodium soy sauce
1 teaspoon sugar
1 teaspoon lemon juice
1 teaspoon dark sesame oil
2 tablespoons vegetable oil, divided
2 teaspoons peeled, minced gingerroot
1 clove garlic, minced
1 cup julienne-sliced sweet red pepper
3 cups julienne-sliced leeks (about 2 large)
2 cups sliced fresh mushrooms
6 cups cooked lo mein noodles or vermicelli
    (cooked without salt or fat)

Peel and devein shrimp; set aside.

Combine chicken broth and next 6 ingredients; stir well, and set aside.

Heat 1 tablespoon vegetable oil in a wok or large nonstick skillet at high (400°) until hot. Add gingerroot and garlic; stir-fry 30 seconds. Add shrimp; stir-fry 2 minutes or until shrimp turn pink. Remove shrimp mixture from wok, and set aside.

Heat remaining 1 tablespoon vegetable oil in wok at medium-high (375°) until hot. Add sweet red pepper, and stir-fry 30 seconds. Add leeks, and stir-fry 1 minute. Add mushrooms, and stir-fry 30 seconds.

Add broth mixture; bring to a boil, and cook, stirring constantly, 1 minute or until thickened. Return shrimp mixture to wok, and cook 1 minute or until thoroughly heated.

For each serving, spoon 1 cup shrimp mixture over 1 cup noodles. Yield: 6 servings.

PER SERVING: 404 CALORIES (19% FROM FAT)
FAT 8.4G (SATURATED FAT 1.5G)
PROTEIN 28.3G   CARBOHYDRATE 51.1G
CHOLESTEROL 151MG   SODIUM 302MG

Spicy Shrimp and Okra

SPICY SHRIMP AND OKRA

2 tablespoons no-salt-added tomato sauce
½ teaspoon extra-spicy salt-free herb and spice
    blend
½ teaspoon dried basil
¼ teaspoon dried oregano
¼ teaspoon salt
½ pound fresh okra pods
1 pound unpeeled medium-size fresh shrimp
Vegetable cooking spray
2 cloves garlic, minced
1½ teaspoons vegetable oil
½ cup diagonally sliced celery
½ cup (1-inch pieces) green pepper
½ cup (1-inch pieces) sweet red pepper
⅓ cup sliced green onions
4 cups cooked rice (cooked without salt or fat)
Fresh basil sprigs (optional)

Combine first 5 ingredients in a bowl; set aside.
Remove tip and stem ends from okra; cut okra
into ¼-inch slices, and set aside.
Peel and devein shrimp. Coat a wok or large nonstick skillet with cooking spray; heat at medium-
high (375°) until hot. Add shrimp and garlic; stir-fry
2 to 3 minutes or until shrimp begin to turn pink.
Add oil, okra, celery, and next 3 ingredients; stir-fry
2 minutes or until vegetables are crisp-tender.
Add tomato sauce mixture to wok; cook 30 seconds, stirring constantly. For each serving, spoon 1
cup shrimp mixture over 1 cup rice. Garnish with
basil sprigs, if desired. Yield: 4 servings.

PER SERVING: 365 CALORIES (9% FROM FAT)
FAT 3.8G (SATURATED FAT 0.7G)
PROTEIN 23.2G CARBOHYDRATE 57.7G
CHOLESTEROL 129MG SODIUM 295MG

FYI

To butterfly shrimp, slit the back of the
shrimp, using a paring knife. Cut almost
through the shrimp. Spread it open, and flatten with the flat side of a knife.

SPICY WALNUT SHRIMP

1 pound unpeeled large fresh shrimp
3 tablespoons dry sherry, divided
1 tablespoon peeled, grated gingerroot
2 teaspoons cornstarch
⅓ cup canned no-salt-added chicken broth,
    undiluted
2 tablespoons low-sodium soy sauce
2 tablespoons low-sodium ketchup
1 tablespoon rice wine vinegar
2 teaspoons sugar
1 teaspoon dark sesame oil
¼ teaspoon ground red pepper
Vegetable cooking spray
2 tablespoons chopped walnuts
1 teaspoon peanut oil
1 (10-ounce) package washed and trimmed
    fresh spinach
1 large clove garlic, minced
1 large sweet red pepper, cut into ½-inch-wide
    strips
2 tablespoons water
6 green onions, cut into 1-inch pieces

Peel, devein, and butterfly shrimp. Combine
shrimp, 1½ tablespoons sherry, and gingerroot.
Cover; marinate in refrigerator 30 to 45 minutes.
Combine remaining 1½ tablespoons sherry, cornstarch, and next 7 ingredients in a small bowl; stir
well, and set aside.
Coat a wok or large nonstick skillet with cooking
spray. Heat at medium-high (375°) until hot. Add
walnuts, and stir-fry 30 seconds. Remove walnuts
from wok, and set aside.
Add peanut oil to wok. Add spinach, and stir-fry
2 minutes. Remove to a serving platter; keep warm.
Add garlic to wok; stir-fry 10 seconds. Add sweet
red pepper and 2 tablespoons water; stir-fry 2 minutes. Add shrimp mixture and green onions; stir-fry
3 to 4 minutes. Add cornstarch mixture; cook, stirring constantly, until mixture is slightly thickened
and bubbly. Spoon over spinach, and sprinkle with
walnuts. Serve immediately. Yield: 4 servings.

PER SERVING: 215 CALORIES (29% FROM FAT)
FAT 7.0G (SATURATED FAT 0.9G)
PROTEIN 26.7G CARBOHYDRATE 10.8G
CHOLESTEROL 172MG SODIUM 426MG

SESAME SHRIMP OVER COUSCOUS

1 pound unpeeled medium-size fresh shrimp
1 cup sliced green onions
2 tablespoons low-sodium soy sauce
1 tablespoon dark sesame oil
1 teaspoon peeled, grated gingerroot
3 cloves garlic, minced
3½ cups canned no-salt-added chicken broth, divided
1½ cups couscous, uncooked
Vegetable cooking spray
2 cups fresh broccoli flowerets
1 cup julienne-sliced sweet red pepper
1 cup fresh snow pea pods, trimmed
2 teaspoons cornstarch
1 teaspoon sesame seeds, toasted

Peel and devein shrimp. Combine shrimp, green onions, and next 4 ingredients in a bowl. Cover and marinate in refrigerator 30 minutes.

Bring 3 cups chicken broth to a boil in a medium saucepan; remove from heat. Stir in couscous; cover and let stand 5 minutes. Fluff couscous with a fork; set aside, and keep warm.

Coat a wok or large nonstick skillet with cooking spray, and heat at medium-high (375°) until hot. Add shrimp mixture; stir-fry 4 minutes or until shrimp turn pink. Remove from wok, and set aside.

Add broccoli, sweet red pepper, and snow peas to wok; stir-fry 3 minutes at medium-high. Combine cornstarch and remaining ½ cup chicken broth; stir well. Add cornstarch mixture to wok; bring to a boil, stirring constantly. Cook 1 minute or until slightly thickened.

Stir in shrimp mixture, and cook 1 minute or until thoroughly heated. For each serving, spoon 1 cup shrimp mixture over 1 cup couscous, and sprinkle with ¼ teaspoon toasted sesame seeds. Yield: 4 servings.

PER SERVING: 402 CALORIES (13% FROM FAT)
FAT 5.8G (SATURATED FAT 0.9G)
PROTEIN 28.1G CARBOHYDRATE 55.5G
CHOLESTEROL 129MG SODIUM 344MG

SZECHUAN NOODLES AND SHRIMP

1 pound unpeeled medium-size fresh shrimp
½ cup reduced-calorie ketchup
¼ cup sugar
¼ cup canned no-salt-added chicken broth, undiluted
2 tablespoons chili puree with garlic
1 tablespoon red wine vinegar
1 tablespoon low-sodium soy sauce
1 teaspoon peeled, minced gingerroot
1½ teaspoons dark sesame oil
⅛ teaspoon pepper
2 cloves garlic, minced
6 ounces egg noodles, uncooked
4 ounces fresh shiitake mushrooms
Vegetable cooking spray
1 teaspoon hot chile oil
1 teaspoon vegetable oil
2 cups julienne-sliced snow pea pods
1 cup diced sweet red pepper

Peel and devein shrimp; set aside.

Combine ketchup and next 9 ingredients in a bowl, stirring well. Add shrimp. Cover and marinate in refrigerator 30 minutes.

Cook noodles according to package directions, omitting salt and fat. Set aside, and keep warm.

Remove and discard mushroom stems; slice mushroom caps.

Coat a wok or large nonstick skillet with cooking spray; add chile and vegetable oils, and heat at medium-high (375°) until hot. Add mushrooms, snow peas, and sweet red pepper; stir-fry 2 to 3 minutes or until crisp-tender.

Add shrimp and marinade to wok; stir-fry 3 to 4 minutes or until shrimp turn pink. Add noodles, and stir-fry 1 minute or until thoroughly heated. Serve immediately. Yield: 4 (1½-cup) servings.

PER SERVING: 405 CALORIES (17% FROM FAT)
FAT 7.8G (SATURATED FAT 1.4G)
PROTEIN 25.6G CARBOHYDRATE 56.9G
CHOLESTEROL 170MG SODIUM 593MG

Gingered Shrimp Linguine

GINGERED SHRIMP LINGUINE

1½ pounds unpeeled large fresh shrimp
1 tablespoon vegetable oil
3 tablespoons peeled, julienne-sliced
    gingerroot
2 cloves garlic, minced
1 cup dry white wine
3 tablespoons white wine Worcestershire
    sauce
¾ cup julienne-sliced sweet red pepper
4 cups shredded Chinese cabbage
3 cups cooked linguine (cooked without salt
    or fat)

Peel and devein shrimp; set aside.

Heat oil in a wok or large nonstick skillet at medium-high (375°) until hot. Add gingerroot and garlic; stir-fry 1 minute. Add wine and Worcestershire sauce to wok; cook 6 minutes or until reduced to ½ cup. Add shrimp and sweet red pepper; cook at medium (350°) for 4 minutes, stirring frequently. Stir in cabbage; cover and cook 2 minutes. For each serving, spoon 1 cup shrimp mixture over ½ cup linguine. Yield: 6 servings.

PER SERVING: 230 CALORIES (17% FROM FAT)
FAT 4.4G (SATURATED FAT 0.8G)
PROTEIN 21.8G   CARBOHYDRATE 24.9G
CHOLESTEROL 129MG   SODIUM 235MG

NOODLE NESTS WITH SHRIMP AND PORK

(pictured on page 28)

6 ounces Chinese egg noodles, uncooked
2 teaspoons light-colored sesame oil
Vegetable cooking spray
1 tablespoon cornstarch
1 tablespoon dry sherry
½ pound unpeeled small fresh shrimp
½ pound lean boneless pork loin, cut into thin strips
½ cup canned no-salt-added beef broth, undiluted
2 teaspoons cornstarch
2 teaspoons low-sodium soy sauce
1 teaspoon oyster sauce
2 teaspoons peanut oil
1 cup sliced green onions
1 cup sliced fresh mushrooms
2 cups julienne-sliced snow pea pods
1 (8-ounce) can sliced water chestnuts, drained
1 teaspoon dried crushed red pepper
Julienne-sliced snow pea pods (optional)
Dried crushed red pepper (optional)

Cook noodles according to package directions, omitting salt and fat; drain. Toss noodles with sesame oil; chill. Shape noodles into 6 (4-inch) rounds on a baking sheet coated with cooking spray; press to make an indentation in center of each round. Bake at 400° for 35 minutes or until golden. Set aside.

Combine 1 tablespoon cornstarch and sherry in a medium bowl; set aside. Peel and devein shrimp. Add shrimp and pork to cornstarch mixture, and toss gently. Cover and marinate in refrigerator 30 minutes.

Combine broth and next 3 ingredients; set aside.

Coat a wok or large nonstick skillet with cooking spray; add peanut oil, and heat at medium-high (375°) until hot. Add shrimp mixture; stir-fry 3 minutes or until shrimp turn pink and pork is done. Remove from wok; set aside.

Add onions and mushrooms to wok; stir-fry 2 minutes. Add 2 cups snow peas, water chestnuts, and 1 teaspoon crushed red pepper. Stir-fry 2 minutes or until crisp-tender. Add shrimp mixture and broth mixture to wok; stir-fry 1 minute or until thickened. Place a noodle nest on each serving plate. Top evenly with shrimp mixture. If desired, garnish with julienne-sliced snow peas and crushed red pepper. Yield: 6 servings.

PER SERVING: 267 CALORIES (27% FROM FAT)
FAT 7.9G (SATURATED FAT 1.8G)
PROTEIN 19.0G   CARBOHYDRATE 29.1G
CHOLESTEROL 93MG   SODIUM 146MG

SHRIMP AND PASTA STIR-FRY

½ pound unpeeled medium-size fresh shrimp
¼ cup nonfat mayonnaise
¼ cup canned low-sodium chicken broth, undiluted
1 teaspoon grated lemon rind
1 tablespoon fresh lemon juice
Vegetable cooking spray
2 teaspoons vegetable oil
1 tablespoon peeled, grated gingerroot
1 clove garlic, minced
1 cup (1-inch) diagonally sliced fresh asparagus (about ½ pound)
2 cups hot cooked penne (short tubular pasta), cooked without salt or fat
¼ teaspoon lemon-pepper seasoning

Peel and devein shrimp; set aside.

Combine mayonnaise and next 3 ingredients in a bowl; stir well with a wire whisk, and set aside.

Coat a wok or large nonstick skillet with cooking spray; add oil, and heat at medium-high (375°) until hot. Add gingerroot and garlic; stir-fry 1 minute. Add shrimp and asparagus; stir-fry 3 minutes or until shrimp turn pink. Add mayonnaise mixture and pasta; cook until heated. Sprinkle with lemon-pepper seasoning. Yield: 2 (1½-cup) servings.

PER SERVING: 403 CALORIES (18% FROM FAT)
FAT 8.2G (SATURATED FAT 1.4G)
PROTEIN 32.1G   CARBOHYDRATE 49.9G
CHOLESTEROL 172MG   SODIUM 570MG

Shrimp and Pasta Stir-Fry

Sizzling Steak Fajitas (recipe on page 67)

HEARTY MEAT DISHES

*O*ne of the best ways to enjoy meat and still reduce fat in your diet is to combine the meat with low-fat, high-carbohydrate items like rice and vegetables. A stir-fry dish offers the perfect solution—it is loaded with flavor and nutrition yet contains little fat.

For Oriental flavor, try Quick Beef with Broccoli (page 59), which is one of the easiest recipes in the chapter. For tastes from other parts of the globe, prepare Sesame-Pork Fajitas (page 80), Curried Lamb (page 73), or Garden Fettuccine with Veal (page 70)—a one-dish meal with a distinctly Italian flavor.

Beef and Asparagus Stir-Fry

BEEF AND ASPARAGUS STIR-FRY

1 pound lean boneless top round steak
3 tablespoons dry sherry
2 tablespoons low-sodium soy sauce
1 teaspoon peeled, minced gingerroot
2 cloves garlic, minced
¾ pound fresh asparagus spears
Vegetable cooking spray
2 teaspoons vegetable oil, divided
1 small carrot, scraped and cut into very thin
     strips
1 stalk celery, cut into very thin strips
½ small onion, sliced and separated into rings
1½ teaspoons cornstarch
2 cups cooked rice (cooked without salt or fat)

Trim fat from steak. Slice steak diagonally across grain into ¼-inch strips. Combine steak and next 4 ingredients in a shallow dish; stir. Cover and marinate in refrigerator 2 to 4 hours, stirring occasionally.

Remove steak from marinade, reserving marinade; set steak and marinade aside.

Snap off tough ends of asparagus. Remove scales from stalks with a knife, if desired. Cut spears into 1-inch pieces, and set aside.

Coat a wok or nonstick skillet with cooking spray. Add 1 teaspoon oil, and heat at high (400°) until hot. Add asparagus, carrot, celery, and onion; stir-fry 3 minutes. Remove vegetables, and set aside.

Add remaining 1 teaspoon oil to wok; add steak,

and stir-fry 2 minutes. Combine cornstarch and reserved marinade, stirring well. Add marinade mixture and vegetables to steak in wok; cook 1 minute or until mixture is thickened and thoroughly heated. Serve over rice. Yield: 4 servings.

PER SERVING: 337 CALORIES (20% FROM FAT)
FAT 7.4G (SATURATED FAT 2.2G)
PROTEIN 30.9G   CARBOHYDRATE 34.4G
CHOLESTEROL 65MG   SODIUM 275MG

TERIYAKI BEEF AND BROCCOLI

(pictured on cover)

¼ cup low-sodium soy sauce
2 tablespoons unsweetened pineapple juice
2 teaspoons cornstarch
1 teaspoon minced garlic
¾ pound lean round steak
Vegetable cooking spray
2 teaspoons vegetable oil
1 medium-size sweet red pepper, seeded and cut into thin strips
1 medium-size sweet yellow pepper, seeded and cut into thin strips
1 cup fresh broccoli flowerets
2 cups cooked rice (cooked without salt or fat)

Combine first 4 ingredients in a small bowl; stir well, and set aside.

Trim fat from steak; slice steak diagonally across grain into ¼-inch-wide strips.

Coat a wok or large nonstick skillet with cooking spray; add oil, and heat at medium-high (375°) until hot. Add steak; stir-fry 2 minutes. Add peppers and broccoli, and stir-fry 4 minutes or until steak is browned. Add reserved cornstarch mixture to steak mixture. Cook, stirring constantly, until thickened. Serve over rice. Yield: 4 servings.

PER SERVING: 280 CALORIES (23% FROM FAT)
FAT 7.0G (SATURATED FAT 2.0G)
PROTEIN 21.8G   CARBOHYDRATE 29.7G
CHOLESTEROL 49MG   SODIUM 444MG

BEEF AND BROCCOLI WITH OYSTER SAUCE

(pictured on page 87)

3 tablespoons oyster sauce
1 tablespoon low-sodium soy sauce
1 tablespoon dry sherry
1 tablespoon water
2 teaspoons sugar
1 teaspoon cornstarch
1 pound lean flank steak
1 tablespoon cornstarch
2 tablespoons water
1 tablespoon low-sodium soy sauce
2 teaspoons sugar
1 tablespoon vegetable oil, divided
⅓ cup (½-inch) diagonally sliced green onions
1 tablespoon peeled, minced gingerroot
6 cups fresh broccoli flowerets (about 1 pound)
¼ cup water
6 cups cooked rice (cooked without salt or fat)

Combine first 6 ingredients, stirring well; set oyster sauce mixture aside.

Trim fat from steak. Slice steak diagonally across grain into thin slices. Combine 1 tablespoon cornstarch, 2 tablespoons water, 1 tablespoon soy sauce, and 2 teaspoons sugar in a medium bowl, stirring well; add steak, stirring to coat. Cover and marinate in refrigerator 15 minutes.

Heat 2 teaspoons oil in a wok or large nonstick skillet at high (400°) until hot. Add steak mixture; stir-fry 2 minutes. Remove steak from wok; set aside. Reduce heat to medium-high (375°). Add remaining 1 teaspoon oil, green onions, and gingerroot to wok; stir-fry 30 seconds. Stir in broccoli and ¼ cup water; cover and cook 3 minutes.

Return steak to wok, and stir in oyster sauce mixture; stir-fry 2 minutes or until thickened. For each serving, spoon 1 cup beef mixture over 1 cup rice. Yield: 6 servings.

PER SERVING: 424 CALORIES (21% FROM FAT)
FAT 9.9G (SATURATED FAT 3.5G)
PROTEIN 22.2G   CARBOHYDRATE 60.4G
CHOLESTEROL 38MG   SODIUM 505MG

Quick Beef with Broccoli

QUICK BEEF WITH BROCCOLI

¾ ounce sun-dried tomatoes (about 10), packed without oil
½ cup boiling water
½ pound lean boneless top round steak
Vegetable cooking spray
½ teaspoon vegetable oil
2 cups fresh broccoli flowerets
¼ cup sliced green onions
1 clove garlic, minced
2 teaspoons cornstarch
¼ cup plus 2 tablespoons dry white wine
¼ cup low-sodium soy sauce
2 cups cooked rice (cooked without salt or fat)

Combine tomatoes and water; let stand 5 minutes. Drain; slice thinly, and set aside.

Trim fat from steak. Slice steak diagonally across grain into thin strips; set aside.

Coat a wok or large nonstick skillet with cooking spray; heat at medium-high (375°) until hot. Add steak; stir-fry 2 minutes. Remove steak from wok; set aside, and keep warm.

Add oil to wok, and heat until hot; add broccoli, and stir-fry 3 minutes. Add tomato, green onions, and garlic; stir-fry 1 minute.

Combine cornstarch, wine, and soy sauce; mix well. Add cornstarch mixture and steak to wok; cook, stirring constantly, 1 minute or until sauce is thickened and bubbly. For each serving, spoon 1 cup steak mixture over 1 cup rice. Yield: 2 servings.

PER SERVING: 474 CALORIES (14% FROM FAT)
FAT 7.6G (SATURATED FAT 2.2G)
PROTEIN 35.5G CARBOHYDRATE 62.5G
CHOLESTEROL 72MG SODIUM 1081MG

STIR-FRIED BEEF AND GREENS

1 pound lean boneless top sirloin steak
¼ cup low-sodium soy sauce
¼ cup canned no-salt-added beef broth, undiluted
¼ cup molasses
2 teaspoons ground ginger
2 teaspoons dry mustard
1 pound fresh mustard greens
2 tablespoons cornstarch
Vegetable cooking spray
1 teaspoon vegetable oil
1 medium-size sweet red pepper, seeded and cut into thin strips
¼ teaspoon dried crushed red pepper
¼ cup water

Trim fat from steak. Slice steak diagonally across grain into ¼-inch-wide strips. Combine soy sauce and next 4 ingredients in a heavy-duty, zip-top plastic bag. Add steak; seal bag, and shake until steak is coated. Marinate in refrigerator at least 1 hour, turning bag occasionally.

Remove and discard stems from mustard greens; wash leaves thoroughly, and pat dry. Coarsely chop greens; set aside.

Remove steak from marinade, reserving marinade. Combine reserved marinade and cornstarch, stirring well; set aside.

Coat a wok or large nonstick skillet with cooking spray; add oil to wok, and heat at medium-high (375°) until hot. Add steak, and stir-fry 5 minutes. Remove steak from wok; drain and pat dry with paper towels.

Add sweet red pepper and crushed red pepper to wok. Stir-fry 1 minute. Add greens and water. Cover and cook 5 minutes or until greens are tender. Add steak and marinade mixture. Bring to a boil, and stir-fry 1 minute or until slightly thickened. Yield: 4 servings.

PER SERVING: 300 CALORIES (26% FROM FAT)
FAT 8.6G (SATURATED FAT 2.7G)
PROTEIN 29.8G CARBOHYDRATE 24.4G
CHOLESTEROL 79MG SODIUM 479MG

SUKIYAKI

4¼ cups water, divided
5 ounces harusame or other transparent
    noodles, uncooked
¼ cup sugar
¼ cup sake (rice wine)
2 tablespoons low-sodium soy sauce
¼ teaspoon beef-flavored bouillon granules
1 pound lean boneless sirloin steak
Vegetable cooking spray
1 teaspoon vegetable oil
1 cup diagonally sliced carrot
2 medium onions, cut into thin strips
6 green onions, cut into 1½-inch pieces
2 cups sliced fresh mushrooms
4 cups loosely packed fresh spinach (about ½
    pound)
6 ounces soft tofu, cut into ½-inch cubes

Bring 4 cups water to a boil in a large saucepan;
add harusame, and cook 2 minutes. Drain. Using
kitchen shears, cut noodles into 3-inch pieces, and
set aside.

Combine ¼ cup water, sugar, and next 3 ingredients in a bowl; stir well, and set aside.

Trim fat from steak; slice steak diagonally across
grain into very thin strips. Set aside.

Coat a wok or large nonstick skillet with cooking
spray; add 1 teaspoon oil. Heat at medium-high
(375°) until hot. Add steak, and stir-fry 2 to 3 minutes. Add ¼ cup soy sauce mixture and carrot; stir-
fry 1 minute, stirring constantly. Add onion strips
and green onions; stir-fry 3 minutes. Add mushrooms; stir-fry 30 seconds. Add noodles and ¼ cup
soy sauce mixture; stir-fry 2 minutes.

Add spinach, tofu, and remaining soy sauce mixture; toss gently. Serve warm. Yield: 6 (1⅓-cup)
servings.

PER SERVING: 255 CALORIES (22% FROM FAT)
FAT 6.1G (SATURATED FAT 1.7G)
PROTEIN 21.1G CARBOHYDRATE 29.6G
CHOLESTEROL 46MG SODIUM 265MG

BEEF AND SPINACH STIR-FRY

1 pound lean flank steak
½ cup boiling water
½ teaspoon beef-flavored bouillon granules
2 tablespoons low-sodium soy sauce
1 teaspoon sugar
1 teaspoon peeled, grated gingerroot
¼ teaspoon dried crushed red pepper
Vegetable cooking spray
2 medium carrots, scraped and shredded
3 green onions, cut into 1-inch pieces
½ pound fresh spinach, coarsely chopped
3 cups cooked rice (cooked without salt or fat)

Trim fat from steak. Slice steak diagonally across
grain into thin strips, and set aside.

Combine water and bouillon granules, stirring
well. Add soy sauce, sugar, gingerroot, and red pepper. Stir well, and set aside.

Coat a wok or large nonstick skillet with cooking
spray. Heat at medium-high (375°) until hot. Add
carrot and green onions; stir-fry 2 minutes. Remove
from wok, and set aside. Add steak to wok; stir-fry
4 minutes or until desired degree of doneness. Add
reserved soy sauce mixture, and bring to a boil.
Cover, reduce heat, and simmer 4 minutes.

Return reserved vegetables and spinach to wok.
Stir-fry 1 minute or until spinach wilts. Serve over
rice. Yield: 6 servings.

PER SERVING: 329 CALORIES (22% FROM FAT)
FAT 7.9G (SATURATED FAT 3.2G)
PROTEIN 22.3G CARBOHYDRATE 44.2G
CHOLESTEROL 38MG SODIUM 341MG

Beef and Spinach Stir-Fry

Beef and Kumquat Stir-Fry

BEEF AND KUMQUAT STIR-FRY

1 tablespoon brown sugar
3 tablespoons low-sodium soy sauce
2 tablespoons hoisin sauce
1 teaspoon dark sesame oil
½ teaspoon ground ginger
3 cloves garlic, crushed
1¼ pounds lean flank steak
⅓ cup sugar
1 cup water
1½ cups fresh kumquats
Vegetable cooking spray
3 cups fresh bean sprouts, divided
2 cups sweet red pepper strips, divided
2 cups green pepper strips, divided
1 cup thinly sliced green onions, divided

Combine first 6 ingredients in a large heavy-duty, zip-top plastic bag. Trim fat from steak; cut steak diagonally across grain into thin slices. Add steak to marinade in bag, turning to coat. Seal bag; marinate in refrigerator 4 hours, turning occasionally.

Combine ⅓ cup sugar and water in a medium saucepan; bring to a boil. Add kumquats; reduce heat, and simmer, uncovered, 10 minutes. Drain; let cool. Cut kumquats in half; set aside.

Coat a wok or large nonstick skillet with cooking spray; heat at medium-high (375°) until hot. Add steak mixture; stir-fry 2 minutes or until desired degree of doneness. Remove steak from wok with a slotted spoon; set aside, and keep warm.

Add half of sprouts, half of red and green pepper strips, and half of green onions to wok; stir-fry 2 minutes. Remove vegetables from wok with a slotted spoon; set aside, and keep warm.

Add remaining sprouts, peppers, and green onions to wok, and stir-fry 2 additional minutes. Combine steak, vegetables, and half of kumquats; toss gently to combine. Arrange on a serving platter; top with remaining kumquats. Yield: 6 (1½-cup) servings.

PER SERVING: 289 CALORIES (32% FROM FAT)
FAT 10.2G (SATURATED FAT 4.0G)
PROTEIN 22.2G CARBOHYDRATE 28.9G
CHOLESTEROL 47MG SODIUM 402MG

GINGERED BEEF AND PINEAPPLE STIR-FRY

1 pound lean flank steak
1 tablespoon peeled, minced gingerroot
2 tablespoons low-sodium soy sauce
2 tablespoons sherry
2 teaspoons sugar
3 cloves garlic, minced
2 teaspoons cornstarch
1 tablespoon plus 1 teaspoon rice vinegar
Vegetable cooking spray
2 teaspoons dark sesame oil
2 cups cubed fresh pineapple
1 cup (3-inch) diagonally sliced green onions
1 cup thinly sliced fresh mushrooms
1 cup fresh snow pea pods (about ¼ pound), trimmed
1 cup julienne-sliced sweet red pepper
6 cups cooked somen (white wheat noodles) or angel hair pasta (cooked without salt or fat)

Trim fat from steak. Cut steak lengthwise with grain into ¼-inch-wide strips; cut strips in half crosswise. Combine steak and next 5 ingredients in a heavy-duty, zip-top plastic bag. Seal bag, and marinate in refrigerator 2 hours, turning bag occasionally. Remove steak from bag; discard marinade.

Combine cornstarch and vinegar; stir well, and set aside.

Coat a wok or large nonstick skillet with cooking spray; add oil, and heat at medium-high (375°) until hot. Add steak; stir-fry 4 minutes. Add reserved cornstarch mixture, pineapple, and next 4 ingredients to wok; stir-fry 3 minutes or until vegetables are crisp-tender. For each serving, spoon 1 cup steak mixture over 1 cup somen noodles. Yield: 6 servings.

PER SERVING: 397 CALORIES (27% FROM FAT)
FAT 11.9G (SATURATED FAT 3.7G)
PROTEIN 23.9G CARBOHYDRATE 52.2G
CHOLESTEROL 38MG SODIUM 143MG

Spicy Beef Fried Rice

SPICY BEEF FRIED RICE

½ cup raisins
½ cup rice vinegar
2 tablespoons tomato sauce
2 tablespoons dry sherry
1 tablespoon oyster sauce
½ teaspoon sugar
¼ teaspoon salt
1 pound lean boneless sirloin steak
2 teaspoons chili oil
1 cup chopped sweet red pepper
¼ cup chopped green onions
2 cloves garlic, minced
4 cups cooked rice (cooked without salt or fat)
2 tablespoons pine nuts, toasted

Combine raisins and vinegar in a bowl; let stand 30 minutes. Drain raisins, reserving 2 tablespoons vinegar. Combine reserved vinegar, tomato sauce, and next 4 ingredients; stir well, and set aside.

Trim fat from steak; slice steak diagonally across grain into thin strips. Heat oil in a wok or large nonstick skillet at medium-high (375°) until hot. Add steak, pepper, green onions, and garlic; stir-fry 4 minutes or until steak loses its pink color. Add raisins and rice; stir-fry 2 minutes. Add tomato sauce mixture; stir-fry 1 minute or until thoroughly heated. Remove from heat; add pine nuts, and toss well. Yield: 7 (1-cup) servings.

PER SERVING: 293 CALORIES (21% FROM FAT)
FAT 6.9G (SATURATED FAT 1.7G)
PROTEIN 17.8G CARBOHYDRATE 40.8G
CHOLESTEROL 40MG SODIUM 235MG

BEEF FAJITAS

3 pounds lean boneless round steak
3 (5½-ounce) cans no-salt-added vegetable juice cocktail
⅔ cup lime juice
½ cup chopped fresh cilantro
¼ teaspoon black pepper
¼ teaspoon ground red pepper
2 large cloves garlic, minced
12 (6-inch) flour tortillas
Vegetable cooking spray
1 cup sweet red pepper strips
1 cup green pepper strips
1½ cups sliced onion
¾ cup salsa
¾ cup nonfat sour cream

Trim fat from steak; slice steak diagonally across grain into ¼-inch-wide strips. Place steak in a heavy-duty, zip-top plastic bag. Combine vegetable juice cocktail and next 5 ingredients; pour over steak. Seal bag; shake until steak is well coated. Marinate in refrigerator 4 to 6 hours, turning bag occasionally.

Heat tortillas according to package directions. Set aside, and keep warm.

Remove steak from marinade, reserving marinade. Coat a wok or large nonstick skillet with cooking spray; heat at medium-high (375°) until hot. Add steak, and stir-fry until steak is browned. Add reserved marinade, pepper strips, and onion; reduce heat to medium (350°), and simmer until vegetables are crisp-tender.

Remove mixture from wok, using a slotted spoon, and divide evenly among tortillas; roll up tortillas. Top each fajita with 1 tablespoon salsa and 1 tablespoon sour cream. Yield: 12 servings.

PER SERVING: 264 CALORIES (21% FROM FAT)
FAT 6.2G (SATURATED FAT 1.8G)
PROTEIN 22.7G CARBOHYDRATE 31.0G
CHOLESTEROL 48MG SODIUM 57MG

Beef Fajita Salad in Tortilla Basket

BEEF FAJITA SALAD IN TORTILLA BASKET

1 pound lean flank steak
½ cup chopped onion
½ cup tomatillo salsa
1 teaspoon hot sauce
¼ teaspoon chili powder
Vegetable cooking spray
4 (10-inch) flour tortillas
1 teaspoon chili powder
1 cup shredded lettuce
2 cups seeded, diced unpeeled tomato
½ cup nonfat sour cream
½ cup Mock Guacamole
¼ cup sliced green onions

Trim fat from steak; cut steak diagonally across grain into thin slices. Combine steak, onion, and next 3 ingredients in a heavy-duty, zip-top plastic bag. Seal bag; marinate in refrigerator 30 minutes to 1 hour.

Place 4 (10-ounce) custard cups upside-down on a baking sheet; coat the bottom of each cup with cooking spray. Lightly coat both sides of tortillas with cooking spray; sprinkle 1 teaspoon chili powder evenly over both sides of tortillas. Place each tortilla over the bottom of a cup, shaping the tortillas around the cups to form baskets. Bake at 375° for 10 minutes or until tortillas are crisp. Set aside; let cool.

Coat a wok or large nonstick skillet with cooking spray; heat at medium-high (375°) until hot. Add steak mixture, and stir-fry 3 minutes or until desired degree of doneness.

To serve, place ¼ cup shredded lettuce, ¾ cup steak mixture, and ½ cup diced tomato into each tortilla basket. Top each with 2 tablespoons sour cream and 2 tablespoons Mock Guacamole. Sprinkle each serving with 1 tablespoon sliced green onions. Yield: 4 servings.

MOCK GUACAMOLE

4 green onions, cut into 1-inch pieces
1 (15-ounce) can small early peas, drained
¼ cup nonfat sour cream
2 tablespoons tomatillo salsa
1 teaspoon olive oil

Position knife blade in food processor bowl; add green onions and peas. Process until blended. Add sour cream, salsa, and oil; process until blended. Spoon into a bowl; cover and chill. Yield: 1½ cups.

PER SERVING: 442 CALORIES (35% FROM FAT)
FAT 17.2G (SATURATED FAT 6.1G)
PROTEIN 30.3G CARBOHYDRATE 38.1G
CHOLESTEROL 60MG SODIUM 607MG

SIZZLING STEAK FAJITAS

(pictured on page 54)

¾ pound lean flank steak
2 teaspoons ground cumin
2 teaspoons chili powder
¼ teaspoon salt
⅛ teaspoon garlic powder
⅛ teaspoon black pepper
⅛ teaspoon ground red pepper
4 (8-inch) flour tortillas
1 teaspoon vegetable oil
2 cups sliced onion
⅓ cup green pepper strips
⅓ cup sweet red pepper strips
⅓ cup sweet yellow pepper strips
1 tablespoon lime juice
¼ cup nonfat sour cream
Green salsa (optional)
Fresh cilantro sprigs (optional)

Trim fat from steak. Slice steak diagonally across grain into thin strips. Combine steak, cumin, and next 5 ingredients in a heavy-duty, zip-top plastic bag; seal bag, and shake well to coat.
Heat tortillas according to package directions; set aside, and keep warm.
Heat oil in a wok or large nonstick skillet at medium-high (375°) until hot. Add steak, onion,

and peppers; stir-fry 6 minutes or until steak is done. Remove from heat; stir in lime juice. Divide mixture evenly among tortillas; roll up. Top each with 1 tablespoon sour cream. If desired, garnish with green salsa and cilantro. Yield: 4 servings.

PER SERVING: 330 CALORIES (34% FROM FAT)
FAT 12.6G (SATURATED FAT 4.2G)
PROTEIN 22.6G CARBOHYDRATE 31.0G
CHOLESTEROL 43MG SODIUM 425MG

STEAK AND PEPPER TORTILLAS

6 ounces lean boneless sirloin steak
1 clove garlic, minced
¼ cup plus 1 tablespoon commercial fat-free
   Italian dressing
½ medium-size sweet red pepper, thinly sliced
   into 2-inch strips
½ medium-size green pepper, thinly sliced into
   2-inch strips
½ cup slivered onion
2 (8-inch) flour tortillas
Vegetable cooking spray

Trim fat from steak. Slice steak diagonally across grain into thin strips; set aside.
Combine garlic and dressing in a medium bowl; stir well. Combine steak and 3 tablespoons dressing mixture in a shallow dish. Cover and marinate in refrigerator 2 hours. Add red and green pepper strips and onion to remaining dressing mixture, tossing well; cover and marinate in refrigerator 2 hours.
Heat tortillas according to package directions; set aside, and keep warm.
Coat a wok or large nonstick skillet with cooking spray; heat at medium-high (375°) until hot. Add steak mixture to wok, and stir-fry 3 minutes. Add pepper mixture to wok, and stir-fry 2 minutes. Spoon half of steak mixture onto each warm tortilla; roll up tortillas. Yield: 2 servings.

PER SERVING: 300 CALORIES (24% FROM FAT)
FAT 7.9G (SATURATED FAT 2.1G)
PROTEIN 22.8G CARBOHYDRATE 33.4G
CHOLESTEROL 52MG SODIUM 578MG

OPEN-FACED STEAK SANDWICHES

½ pound lean boneless sirloin steak
Vegetable cooking spray
¾ cup sliced fresh mushrooms
½ small onion, separated into rings
¼ teaspoon minced garlic
1½ tablespoons low-sodium Worcestershire
    sauce
1½ teaspoons cornstarch
½ cup canned no-salt-added beef broth,
    undiluted
⅛ teaspoon dried basil
⅛ teaspoon pepper
Dash of salt
Dash of dry mustard
4 (¾-ounce) slices French bread, toasted

Trim fat from steak. Slice steak diagonally across grain into ⅛-inch-wide strips. Coat a wok or non-stick skillet with cooking spray. Heat at medium-high (375°) until hot. Add steak; stir-fry 3 minutes or until browned. Drain and pat steak dry with paper towels. Wipe drippings from wok with a paper towel.

Coat wok with cooking spray. Heat at medium-high until hot. Add mushrooms, onion, and garlic; stir-fry until tender. Combine Worcestershire sauce and cornstarch in a small bowl, stirring until smooth. Stir in beef broth and next 4 ingredients. Add broth mixture to mushroom mixture, and cook at medium (350°), stirring constantly, 2 minutes or until mixture is thickened. Add steak, and cook 2 to 3 minutes or until thoroughly heated.

To serve, place 2 bread slices on each serving plate; spoon beef mixture evenly over bread. Serve immediately. Yield: 2 servings.

PER SERVING: 361 CALORIES (21% FROM FAT)
FAT 8.6G (SATURATED FAT 2.9G)
PROTEIN 32.8G CARBOHYDRATE 35.4G
CHOLESTEROL 81MG SODIUM 466MG

VEAL AND ASPARAGUS STIR-FRY

½ pound fresh asparagus spears
1 pound veal cutlets (¼ inch thick)
Vegetable cooking spray
1 teaspoon vegetable oil
1 small onion, thinly sliced
1 small sweet red pepper, seeded and cut into
    ¼-inch strips
¼ teaspoon salt
¼ teaspoon fennel seeds, crushed
⅛ teaspoon garlic powder
⅛ teaspoon dried crushed red pepper
2 tablespoons dry sherry
1 teaspoon lemon zest

Snap off tough ends of asparagus. Remove scales from stalks with a knife or vegetable peeler, if desired. Cut asparagus into 2-inch pieces. Set aside.

Trim fat from cutlets; cut into thin strips.

Coat a wok or large nonstick skillet with cooking spray; add oil, and heat at medium-high (375°) until hot. Add veal; stir-fry 5 minutes or until browned. Remove veal from wok with a slotted spoon, and set aside.

Add reserved asparagus, onion, and next 5 ingredients to wok; stir-fry 3 to 4 minutes or until vegetables are crisp-tender. Return veal to wok. Add sherry, and cook, stirring constantly, 1 minute or until thoroughly heated. Spoon onto a platter, and sprinkle with lemon zest. Yield: 4 servings.

PER SERVING: 168 CALORIES (26% FROM FAT)
FAT 4.8G (SATURATED FAT 1.2G)
PROTEIN 24.3G CARBOHYDRATE 6.6G
CHOLESTEROL 94MG SODIUM 248MG

Veal and Asparagus Stir-Fry

GARDEN FETTUCCINE WITH VEAL

½ pound veal cutlets, cut into very thin strips
¼ teaspoon garlic powder
¼ teaspoon dried basil
Olive oil-flavored vegetable cooking spray
1 cup fresh broccoli flowerets
¾ cup sliced yellow squash
¾ cup sliced zucchini
½ cup julienne-sliced sweet red pepper
½ cup julienne-sliced sweet yellow pepper
½ cup sliced green onions

1 cup peeled, chopped tomato
¾ cup sliced fresh mushrooms
1 teaspoon minced garlic
1 cup canned no-salt-added chicken broth,
     undiluted
1 teaspoon dried Italian seasoning
1 teaspoon dried basil
1 teaspoon coarsely ground pepper
6 ounces fettuccine, uncooked
¼ cup freshly grated Parmesan cheese

Garden Fettuccine with Veal

Combine first 3 ingredients, tossing gently. Coat a wok or large nonstick skillet with cooking spray; heat at medium (350°) until hot. Add veal; cook, stirring constantly, 5 minutes or until browned. Drain and pat dry with paper towels; set aside. Wipe drippings from wok with a paper towel.

Coat wok with cooking spray, and heat wok at medium-high (375°) until hot. Add broccoli and next 5 ingredients; stir-fry vegetables 3 minutes. Add tomato, mushrooms, and garlic; stir-fry 2 minutes. Return veal to wok. Add chicken broth and next 3 ingredients; bring to a boil. Reduce heat, and simmer, uncovered, 15 minutes or until most of liquid evaporates.

Cook pasta according to package directions, omitting salt and fat; drain. Combine pasta and veal mixture in a serving bowl, tossing gently. Sprinkle cheese over mixture, and serve immediately. Yield: 5 (1-cup) servings.

PER SERVING: 260 CALORIES (19% FROM FAT)
FAT 5.4G (SATURATED FAT 1.8G)
PROTEIN 19.7G CARBOHYDRATE 33.4G
CHOLESTEROL 44MG SODIUM 163MG

LAMB AND WHITE BEAN STIR-FRY

½ pound lean boneless leg of lamb
¼ cup no-salt-added tomato juice
1 teaspoon cornstarch
½ teaspoon dried rosemary, crushed
½ teaspoon ground white pepper
Vegetable cooking spray
⅓ cup chopped onion
2 cloves garlic, minced
1 cup drained canned cannellini beans
¾ cup chopped plum tomato

Trim fat from lamb, and cut lamb into thin strips; set aside. Combine tomato juice and next 3 ingredients; stir well, and set aside.

Coat a wok or large nonstick skillet with cooking spray; heat at medium-high (375°) until hot. Add onion and garlic; stir-fry 2 minutes. Add lamb; stir-fry

2 minutes. Add tomato juice mixture; bring to a boil, and cook 30 seconds, stirring constantly. Stir in beans and tomato; cook 1 minute or until thoroughly heated. Yield: 2 (1½-cup) servings.

PER SERVING: 298 CALORIES (20% FROM FAT)
FAT 6.2G (SATURATED FAT 1.9G)
PROTEIN 31.7G CARBOHYDRATE 29.5G
CHOLESTEROL 73MG SODIUM 540MG

MIDDLE EASTERN-STYLE LAMB

½ cup tomato juice
1 tablespoon lemon juice
2 teaspoons cornstarch
1 teaspoon ground cinnamon
¼ teaspoon ground nutmeg
1 pound lean boneless lamb round steak
Vegetable cooking spray
2 cloves garlic, minced
1 large sweet red pepper, chopped
1 medium-size green pepper, chopped
2 tablespoons chopped onion
2 tablespoons pine nuts
2 cups cooked rice (cooked without salt or fat)

Combine first 5 ingredients in a small bowl; stir well, and set aside.

Trim fat from lamb; cut lamb into thin strips, and set aside.

Coat a wok or large nonstick skillet with cooking spray; heat at medium-high (375°) until hot. Add garlic; stir-fry 30 seconds. Add lamb; stir-fry 2 minutes. Add red and green peppers, onion, and pine nuts; stir-fry 2 minutes.

Add reserved tomato juice mixture; bring to a boil, stirring constantly, and cook until thickened. For each serving, spoon ½ cup lamb mixture over ½ cup rice. Yield: 4 servings.

PER SERVING: 340 CALORIES (31% FROM FAT)
FAT 11.6G (SATURATED FAT 3.1G)
PROTEIN 27.2G CARBOHYDRATE 31.9G
CHOLESTEROL 75MG SODIUM 194MG

Lamb Fajitas with Cucumber-Dill Sauce and chick-pea salad

LAMB FAJITAS WITH CUCUMBER-DILL SAUCE

¾ pound lean boneless leg of lamb
1 teaspoon olive oil
½ teaspoon dried oregano
¼ teaspoon salt
¼ teaspoon pepper
2 cloves garlic, minced
4 (8-inch) flour tortillas
1 teaspoon olive oil
¼ cup thinly sliced fresh mint leaves
Cucumber-Dill Sauce
Fresh dill sprigs (optional)

Trim fat from lamb, and cut lamb into thin strips. Combine lamb, 1 teaspoon oil, and next 4 ingredients in a heavy-duty, zip-top plastic bag; seal bag, and shake. Marinate in refrigerator 20 minutes.

Heat tortillas according to package directions; set aside, and keep warm.

Heat 1 teaspoon oil in a wok or large nonstick skillet at medium-high (375°) until hot. Add lamb; stir-fry 6 minutes. Divide lamb evenly among tortillas; sprinkle with mint, and roll up. Serve each fajita with ¼ cup plus 2 tablespoons Cucumber-Dill Sauce. Garnish with dill sprigs, if desired. Yield: 4 servings.

CUCUMBER-DILL SAUCE
1 cup peeled, seeded, and diced cucumber
¼ teaspoon dried dillweed
1 clove garlic, minced
1 (8-ounce) carton plain nonfat yogurt

Combine all ingredients in a small bowl; stir well. Cover and chill. Yield: 1½ cups.

PER SERVING: 324 CALORIES (27% FROM FAT)
FAT 9.6G (SATURATED FAT 2.3G)
PROTEIN 25.3G CARBOHYDRATE 32.8G
CHOLESTEROL 56MG SODIUM 471MG

CURRIED LAMB

Vegetable cooking spray
1 teaspoon vegetable oil
1 cup sliced celery
½ cup chopped onion
¾ pound lean boneless lamb, cut into ½-inch cubes
2 teaspoons curry powder
½ teaspoon salt
⅛ teaspoon ground cloves
½ cup water
¼ cup skim milk
1½ teaspoons cornstarch
2 cups cooked rice (cooked without salt or fat)
1 medium tomato, cut into wedges

Coat a wok or large nonstick skillet with cooking spray; add oil, and heat at medium-high (375°) until hot. Add celery and onion; stir-fry 2 to 3 minutes. Remove vegetables from wok; set aside.

Coat wok with cooking spray; heat at medium-high until hot. Add lamb, and stir-fry 2 minutes or until browned. Remove lamb, and drain on paper towels; wipe wok dry with a paper towel.

Coat wok with cooking spray. Return lamb to wok. Stir in reserved vegetable mixture, curry, salt, and cloves; cook at medium (350°) for 1 minute. Combine water, milk, and cornstarch in a small bowl; stir until well blended. Gradually pour milk mixture into wok, stirring well; bring to a boil, and cook, stirring constantly, 1 minute. Reduce heat to low, and simmer 5 minutes. Serve over rice, and garnish with tomato wedges. Yield: 4 servings.

PER SERVING: 284 CALORIES (24% FROM FAT)
FAT 7.7G (SATURATED FAT 2.4G)
PROTEIN 21.7G CARBOHYDRATE 30.7G
CHOLESTEROL 58MG SODIUM 383MG

Super Salad

For a colorful chick-pea salad, toss drained chick-peas, cherry tomatoes, and purple onions with lemon juice, olive oil, salt, and pepper.

FRIED RICE WITH BOK CHOY, HAM, AND EGG

½ cup water
½ ounce dried shiitake mushrooms
1 tablespoon vegetable oil, divided
½ cup frozen egg substitute, thawed
1 teaspoon peeled, minced gingerroot
2 cloves garlic, minced
2 cups julienne-sliced bok choy
¼ pound lean, lower-salt smoked ham, cut into thin 1-inch strips
3 cups cooked rice (cooked without salt or fat)
¼ cup canned no-salt-added chicken broth, undiluted
¼ teaspoon salt
¼ teaspoon pepper

Combine ½ cup water and mushrooms in a saucepan, and bring to a boil; remove from heat. Cover; let stand 30 minutes. Drain mushrooms, reserving 3 tablespoons cooking liquid. Remove and discard stems. Chop mushroom caps, and set aside.

Heat 1 teaspoon oil in a large nonstick skillet over medium-high heat. Add egg substitute; tilt skillet so egg substitute covers bottom. Cook 1½ minutes or until set. Remove egg; cut into 1-inch strips. Set aside.

Heat remaining 2 teaspoons oil in skillet. Add gingerroot and garlic; stir-fry 30 seconds. Add mushroom caps, bok choy, and ham; stir-fry 1 minute. Add rice; stir-fry 2 minutes. Add reserved mushroom cooking liquid, egg strips, broth, salt, and pepper. Increase heat to high, and stir-fry 2 minutes or until liquid is nearly absorbed. Yield: 5 (1-cup) servings.

PER SERVING: 216 CALORIES (17% FROM FAT)
FAT 4.1G (SATURATED FAT 0.9G)
PROTEIN 9.8G CARBOHYDRATE 34.0G
CHOLESTEROL 11MG SODIUM 348MG

ORIENTAL PORK AND EGGPLANT

1 (1¼-pound) eggplant, peeled and cut
    crosswise into 12 (½-inch) slices
1 tablespoon plus 1 teaspoon vegetable oil,
    divided
1½ pounds pork tenderloin
¼ cup coarsely shredded carrot
¼ cup chopped canned water chestnuts
¼ cup diced sweet red pepper
3 tablespoons rice wine vinegar
2 tablespoons minced green onions
1 tablespoon low-sodium soy sauce
1 teaspoon peeled, grated gingerroot
½ teaspoon grated orange rind
⅛ teaspoon dried crushed red pepper
1 clove garlic, crushed
1 teaspoon sesame seeds, toasted
Fresh cilantro sprigs (optional)

Arrange eggplant in a single layer on a baking
sheet. Brush slices with 1 tablespoon oil. Bake at
350° for 30 minutes or until tender. Arrange on a
large platter; cover and set aside.

Trim fat from pork, and cut pork into 2- x ⅛-
inch strips. Heat remaining 1 teaspoon oil in a wok
or large nonstick skillet; heat at medium-high
(375°) until hot. Add pork, and stir-fry 4 minutes.

Add carrot and next 9 ingredients to wok, and
cook, stirring constantly, 1 minute. For each serving, spoon ⅔ cup pork mixture over 2 slices eggplant; sprinkle with sesame seeds. Garnish with
fresh cilantro sprigs, if desired. Yield: 6 servings.

PER SERVING: 192 CALORIES (30% FROM FAT)
FAT 6.3G (SATURATED FAT 1.6G)
PROTEIN 25.3G   CARBOHYDRATE 8.2G
CHOLESTEROL 74MG   SODIUM 144MG

PORK AND VEGETABLE LO MEIN

1 pound pork tenderloin
¼ cup low-sodium soy sauce
1 teaspoon peeled, grated gingerroot
¼ teaspoon dried crushed red pepper
3 cloves garlic, crushed
Vegetable cooking spray
2 cups fresh snow pea pods, trimmed
1 cup julienne-sliced sweet red pepper
3 cups cooked vermicelli (cooked without salt
    or fat)
⅓ cup canned low-sodium chicken broth,
    undiluted
2 teaspoons dark sesame oil

Trim fat from pork, and cut tenderloin in half
lengthwise. Cut each half crosswise into ½-inch-
thick slices; set aside.

Combine soy sauce and next 3 ingredients in a
heavy-duty, zip-top plastic bag. Add pork; seal bag,
and marinate in refrigerator 20 minutes.

Coat a wok or large nonstick skillet with cooking
spray; heat at medium-high (375°) until hot. Add
pork mixture; stir-fry 1½ minutes or until browned.
Add snow peas and sweet red pepper; stir-fry 1
minute. Stir in vermicelli and broth; cook 1 minute.
Remove from heat; stir in sesame oil. Spoon onto a
serving platter. Yield: 6 (1-cup) servings.

PER SERVING: 220 CALORIES (17% FROM FAT)
FAT 4.2G (SATURATED FAT 1.0G)
PROTEIN 20.4G   CARBOHYDRATE 23.1G
CHOLESTEROL 49MG   SODIUM 304MG

FYI

Rice vinegar, often used in Asian recipes,
is made from fermented rice wine. The
Japanese version of rice vinegar is mild and
mellow, while the Chinese version is often
slightly sour.

MANGO-PORK STIR-FRY

2 (½-pound) pork tenderloins
¼ cup low-sodium soy sauce
¼ cup dry sherry
2 teaspoons dark sesame oil
¼ cup water
2 teaspoons cornstarch
Vegetable cooking spray
1 tablespoon plus 1 teaspoon vegetable oil
1 cup sweet red pepper strips
1 tablespoon plus 1 teaspoon peeled, minced
    gingerroot
2 large cloves garlic, minced
2 mangoes, peeled and cubed
4 cups cooked basmati rice (cooked without
    salt or fat)
¼ cup sliced green onions

Cut pork crosswise into ¼-inch-thick slices. Combine pork, soy sauce, sherry, and sesame oil in a bowl; stir well. Cover and marinate in refrigerator 30 minutes, stirring occasionally.

Remove pork from marinade, reserving marinade. Combine water and cornstarch; add to reserved marinade, and set aside.

Coat a wok or large nonstick skillet with cooking spray; add vegetable oil, and heat at medium-high (375°) until hot. Add pork; stir-fry 1 minute. Add sweet red pepper, gingerroot, and garlic; stir-fry 2 minutes. Add marinade mixture; bring to a boil, and cook, stirring constantly, 1 minute. Add mango; stir-fry 1 minute. For each serving, spoon 1 cup rice and 1 cup pork mixture onto a plate, and sprinkle with 1 tablespoon sliced green onions. Yield: 4 servings.

PER SERVING: 492 CALORIES (19% FROM FAT)
FAT 10.4G (SATURATED FAT 2.2G)
PROTEIN 28.8G   CARBOHYDRATE 68.2G
CHOLESTEROL 74MG   SODIUM 450MG

Mango-Pork Stir-Fry

ORIENTAL PORK IN LETTUCE WRAPPERS

4 large romaine lettuce leaves
6 ounces pork tenderloin, cut into 2½- x ¼-inch strips
1 teaspoon peeled, grated gingerroot, divided
¼ teaspoon dried crushed red pepper
1 clove garlic, minced
1 tablespoon dry sherry
2 teaspoons rice wine vinegar
2 teaspoons low-sodium soy sauce
1 teaspoon cornstarch
Vegetable cooking spray
1 teaspoon vegetable oil, divided
1 cup coarsely chopped sweet red pepper
2 green onions, diagonally cut into 1-inch pieces

Cut off raised portion of the main vein of each romaine lettuce leaf. Plunge leaves into boiling water for 10 seconds; drain and rinse thoroughly under cold, running water. Set aside.

Combine pork tenderloin, ½ teaspoon gingerroot, crushed red pepper, and minced garlic in a bowl; stir well, and set aside. Combine sherry, vinegar, soy sauce, and cornstarch in a bowl; stir well. Add to pork mixture; stir well.

Coat a wok or large nonstick skillet with cooking spray; add ½ teaspoon oil, and heat at medium-high (375°) until hot. Add sweet red pepper; stir-fry 3 minutes. Add green onions and remaining ½ teaspoon gingerroot; stir-fry 1 minute. Spoon into a bowl; set aside.

Recoat wok with cooking spray; add remaining ½ teaspoon oil, and heat at medium-high until hot. Add pork mixture; stir-fry 4 minutes or until pork is done. Return sweet red pepper mixture to wok; cook 1 minute or until thoroughly heated.

Spoon ½ cup pork mixture onto lower third of each romaine lettuce leaf. Fold sides in, and roll up jellyroll fashion, starting at stem end. Yield: 2 servings.

PER SERVING: 162 CALORIES (30% FROM FAT)
FAT 5.4G (SATURATED FAT 1.2G)
PROTEIN 19.3G   CARBOHYDRATE 8.2G
CHOLESTEROL 55MG   SODIUM 183MG

PORK AND PEPPERS

You may substitute vermicelli for Oriental curly noodles, if desired.

1 (5-ounce) package Oriental curly noodles, uncooked
1 pound pork tenderloin
3 tablespoons low-sodium soy sauce, divided
½ cup unsweetened orange juice
2 tablespoons balsamic vinegar
1 tablespoon honey
2 teaspoons cornstarch
¼ teaspoon freshly ground pepper
Vegetable cooking spray
1½ cups cubed sweet red pepper
1½ cups cubed sweet yellow pepper

Cook noodles according to package directions, omitting salt and fat. Drain and set aside.

Trim fat from pork. Cut pork into ¾-inch cubes. Combine pork and 1 tablespoon soy sauce; stir well, and set aside. Combine remaining 2 tablespoons soy sauce, orange juice, and next 4 ingredients; stir well, and set aside.

Coat a wok or large nonstick skillet with cooking spray; heat at high (400°) until hot. Add pork mixture; stir-fry 1½ minutes or until browned. Remove pork from wok; set aside.

Add red and yellow peppers to wok; stir-fry 2 minutes. Return pork to wok; add juice mixture. Bring to a boil, and cook, stirring constantly, 1 minute. Add noodles; cook 1 minute or until heated. Yield: 4 (1½-cup) servings.

PER SERVING: 346 CALORIES (12% FROM FAT)
FAT 4.5G (SATURATED FAT 1.3G)
PROTEIN 31.0G   CARBOHYDRATE 41.8G
CHOLESTEROL 74MG   SODIUM 377MG

Peachy Pork Stir-Fry

PEACHY PORK STIR-FRY

2 boneless pork chops (about ½ pound)
¼ teaspoon salt
½ teaspoon ground white pepper
⅓ cup low-sugar apricot spread
¼ cup peach nectar
1 tablespoon cornstarch
Vegetable cooking spray
1 teaspoon peeled, minced gingerroot
3 cups peeled, sliced fresh peaches
6 ounces fresh snow pea pods, trimmed

Trim fat from chops; slice chops diagonally across grain into thin strips. Sprinkle with salt and pepper; set aside.

Combine apricot spread, peach nectar, and cornstarch; stir well, and set aside.

Coat a wok or large nonstick skillet with cooking spray; heat at medium-high (375°) until hot. Add gingerroot; stir-fry 30 seconds. Add pork; stir-fry 3 minutes. Add apricot mixture; cook, stirring constantly, 1 minute or until mixture is thickened. Add peaches and snow peas; toss gently. Cover and cook 1 minute or until thoroughly heated. Yield: 3 (2-cup) servings.

PER SERVING: 247 CALORIES (22% FROM FAT)
FAT 5.9G (SATURATED FAT 1.9G)
PROTEIN 19.5G CARBOHYDRATE 34.1G
CHOLESTEROL 48MG SODIUM 253MG

PORK AND PUMPKIN STIR-FRY

5 cups peeled, cubed fresh pumpkin (about 2 pounds)
1 pound lean boneless pork loin, cut into 1-inch pieces
2 tablespoons dry sherry
½ teaspoon peeled, grated gingerroot
1 clove garlic, halved
2 tablespoons water
2 tablespoons low-sodium soy sauce
1 teaspoon cornstarch
¼ teaspoon sugar
1 teaspoon vegetable oil
5 green onions, sliced lengthwise and cut into 1-inch pieces
3 cups cooked rice (cooked without salt or fat)

Combine first 5 ingredients in a bowl; stir well. Cover and marinate in refrigerator 30 minutes.

Combine water and next 3 ingredients; stir well, and set aside.

Heat oil in a wok or large nonstick skillet at medium-high (375°) until hot. Add pork mixture; stir-fry 12 to 15 minutes or until pork is done and pumpkin is tender. Discard garlic. Add green onions; cook 2 minutes, stirring frequently. Add cornstarch mixture; stir well. Cover, reduce heat, and simmer 3 minutes or until slightly thickened. For each serving, spoon 1 cup pork mixture over ½ cup rice. Yield: 6 servings.

PER SERVING: 268 CALORIES (23% FROM FAT)
FAT 6.7G (SATURATED FAT 2.2G)
PROTEIN 18.9G   CARBOHYDRATE 32.2G
CHOLESTEROL 45MG   SODIUM 182MG

SWEET-AND-SOUR PORK

1½ pounds lean boneless pork loin
Vegetable cooking spray
1 (8-ounce) can no-salt-added tomato sauce
¼ cup cider vinegar
2 tablespoons brown sugar
2 teaspoons low-sodium soy sauce
⅛ teaspoon garlic powder
⅛ teaspoon pepper
1 (20-ounce) can pineapple chunks in juice, undrained
1 medium-size green pepper, seeded and cut into 1-inch pieces
1 small onion, thinly sliced
2 tablespoons cornstarch
4 cups cooked rice (cooked without salt or fat)

Trim fat from pork; cut into ½-inch pieces. Coat a large nonstick skillet with cooking spray; place over medium-high heat until hot. Add pork; stir-fry 10 minutes or until browned. Remove pork from skillet; drain and pat dry with paper towels. Wipe drippings from skillet with a paper towel.

Return pork to skillet. Add tomato sauce and next 5 ingredients; bring to a boil. Cover, reduce heat, and simmer 15 minutes or until pork is tender.

Drain pineapple, reserving juice; add enough water to juice to equal 1 cup. Set aside. Add pineapple, green pepper, and onion to skillet; cover and simmer 5 to 7 minutes or until vegetables are crisp-tender.

Combine cornstarch and pineapple juice mixture; stir into pork mixture. Cook, stirring constantly, until thickened and bubbly. Serve over rice. Yield: 8 servings.

PER SERVING: 322 CALORIES (18% FROM FAT)
FAT 6.3G (SATURATED FAT 2.1G)
PROTEIN 21.5G   CARBOHYDRATE 43.6G
CHOLESTEROL 56MG   SODIUM 98MG

Sweet-and-Sour Pork

PORK AND SUGAR SNAP PEAS IN PITAS

½ pound pork tenderloin
1 teaspoon cornstarch
2 teaspoons dry sherry
½ teaspoon low-sodium soy sauce
¼ teaspoon dried crushed red pepper
2 teaspoons vegetable oil, divided
3 cups Sugar Snap peas
2 teaspoons peeled, minced gingerroot
2 cloves garlic, minced
2 cups vertically sliced onion
½ cup chopped pear
1 tablespoon plus 1 teaspoon rice vinegar
1 tablespoon oyster sauce
1 teaspoon dry sherry
¼ teaspoon sugar
⅓ cup chopped fresh cilantro
¼ teaspoon salt
2 (6-inch) pita bread rounds, cut in half
4 curly leaf lettuce leaves

Trim fat from pork, and cut pork into 2- x ¼-inch strips. Combine pork, cornstarch, 2 teaspoons sherry, soy sauce, and red pepper in a bowl; stir well. Cover and marinate in refrigerator 10 minutes.

Heat 1 teaspoon oil in a wok or large nonstick skillet at medium-high (375°) until hot. Add peas, gingerroot, and garlic; stir-fry 2 minutes. Remove from wok, and set aside.

Add remaining 1 teaspoon oil to wok. Add pork mixture, onion, and pear; stir-fry 3 minutes or until pork is browned. Add vinegar, oyster sauce, 1 teaspoon sherry, and sugar; stir-fry 30 seconds. Return pea mixture to wok, and stir in cilantro and salt. Line each pita half with a lettuce leaf, and fill with 1 cup pork mixture. Yield: 4 servings.

PER SERVING: 240 CALORIES (18% FROM FAT)
FAT 4.8G (SATURATED FAT 1.1G)
PROTEIN 17.7G   CARBOHYDRATE 30.7G
CHOLESTEROL 37MG   SODIUM 462MG

SESAME-PORK FAJITAS

1 pound pork tenderloin
2 teaspoons dark sesame oil
1 teaspoon peeled, grated gingerroot
¼ teaspoon salt
¼ teaspoon ground red pepper
2 cloves garlic, minced
4 moo shu shells or flour tortillas
Vegetable cooking spray
¼ cup hoisin sauce

Trim fat from pork, and cut into thin strips. Combine pork, oil, and next 4 ingredients in a heavy-duty, zip-top plastic bag; seal bag, and shake well to coat. Marinate in refrigerator 20 minutes.

Heat shells according to package directions.

Coat a wok or large nonstick skillet with cooking spray; heat at medium-high (375°) until hot. Add pork mixture; stir-fry 4 minutes or until done.

Divide pork mixture evenly among warm moo shu shells. Drizzle hoisin sauce over pork mixture, and roll up. Yield: 4 servings.

PER SERVING: 267 CALORIES (23% FROM FAT)
FAT 6.8G (SATURATED FAT 1.3G)
PROTEIN 26.7G   CARBOHYDRATE 24.0G
CHOLESTEROL 74MG   SODIUM 553MG

PORK AND SUCCOTASH SALAD

4 medium ears fresh corn
1½ cups shelled fresh lima beans
½ pound fresh spinach
1 medium-size sweet red pepper, finely chopped
1 small purple onion, finely chopped
⅛ teaspoon black pepper
1½ teaspoons ground cumin
½ teaspoon garlic powder
½ teaspoon chili powder
½ pound lean boneless pork, cut into thin strips
Vegetable cooking spray
1 cup unsweetened orange juice
1 tablespoon lime juice
1 tablespoon olive oil

Pork and Succotash Salad

Place corn in a Dutch oven, and cover with water. Bring to a boil, and cook 20 minutes or until corn is tender. Drain and cool. Cut corn from cob, and set aside.

Cook beans, uncovered, in boiling water 15 minutes or until tender. Drain beans, and set aside.

Remove stems from spinach, and wash leaves thoroughly. Tear into bite-size pieces. Combine spinach, reserved corn, beans, sweet red pepper, onion, and black pepper in a large bowl. Toss well, and set aside.

Combine cumin, garlic powder, and chili powder in a small bowl, stirring well. Add pork, tossing lightly to coat.

Coat a wok or large nonstick skillet with cooking spray, and heat at medium-high (375°) until hot. Add pork to wok, and cook 3 minutes or until browned, stirring constantly. Remove pork from wok, and drain.

Add orange juice to wok. Scrape bottom of wok to loosen browned spices. Bring to a boil, and cook until orange juice mixture reduces to about ½ cup. Stir in lime juice and oil, mixing well.

Pour juice mixture over reserved salad mixture; add pork, and toss salad well. Serve immediately, or chill. Yield: 4 (2-cup) servings.

PER SERVING: 330 CALORIES (30% FROM FAT)
FAT 11.0G (SATURATED FAT 22.7G)
PROTEIN 21.0G CARBOHYDRATE 40.9G
CHOLESTEROL 39MG SODIUM 94MG

Chicken and Snow Pea Stir-Fry (recipe on page 85)

PERFECT POULTRY

The next time you're in the mood for Chinese food, don't call for take-out—heat up the wok instead! With recipes like Easy Sweet-and-Sour Chicken (page 92) and Chinese Chicken Fried Rice (page 94), all you'll need is green tea and fortune cookies to complete the meal.

Peking Chicken (page 98) is one dish you should certainly try. It's similar in taste to the classic Peking duck but has less fat and fewer calories than does the original recipe.

For other flavors, try Pesto and Chicken (page 95) or Moroccan Chicken and Orzo (page 97). Starting on page 99 are several recipes calling for turkey breast, ground turkey, and even turkey sausage. Some have an Oriental origin while others have their roots in North American cooking.

Chicken Stir-Fry for Two

CHICKEN STIR-FRY FOR TWO

2 (4-ounce) skinned, boned chicken breast
    halves
Vegetable cooking spray
1 teaspoon sesame oil
1 cup fresh broccoli flowerets
1 cup sliced fresh mushrooms
¼ cup chopped green onions
2 teaspoons minced garlic
¾ cup fresh bean sprouts
¾ cup fresh snow pea pods, trimmed
¼ cup canned sliced water chestnuts, drained
½ cup canned low-sodium chicken broth,
    undiluted
1 tablespoon dry sherry
1 tablespoon low-sodium soy sauce
1 teaspoon cornstarch
⅛ teaspoon salt
2 cups cooked rice (cooked without salt or fat)

Cut chicken into ¼-inch-wide strips.

Coat a wok or medium nonstick skillet with cooking spray; add oil. Heat at medium-high (375°) until hot. Add chicken, and stir-fry 2 minutes. Add broccoli and next 3 ingredients; stir-fry 2 minutes. Add bean sprouts, snow peas, and water chestnuts; stir-fry 1 minute.

Combine chicken broth and next 4 ingredients, stirring well; add to chicken mixture. Cook, stirring constantly, until mixture is slightly thickened and thoroughly heated. Spoon chicken mixture over cooked rice. Yield: 2 servings.

PER SERVING: 439 CALORIES (10% FROM FAT)
FAT 5.0G (SATURATED FAT 0.9G)
PROTEIN 34.9G   CARBOHYDRATE 61.4G
CHOLESTEROL 66MG   SODIUM 448MG

LEMON CHICKEN STIR-FRY

1½ pounds skinned, boned chicken breast
    halves
¼ cup water
2 tablespoons low-sodium soy sauce
1 teaspoon grated lemon rind
¼ cup lemon juice
¼ teaspoon chicken-flavored bouillon
    granules
1 tablespoon sugar
1 tablespoon cornstarch
Vegetable cooking spray
1 teaspoon vegetable oil
3 medium carrots, scraped and cut into very
    thin strips
4 green onions, cut into 2-inch pieces
1 medium-size green pepper, seeded and cut
    into strips
1 medium-size sweet red pepper, seeded and
    cut into strips
3 cups cooked rice (cooked without salt or fat)

Cut chicken into 1-inch pieces, and place in a shallow container. Combine water and next 4 ingredients, stirring well; pour over chicken, turning to coat. Cover and marinate in refrigerator 30 minutes.

Drain chicken, reserving marinade; combine marinade, sugar, and cornstarch, stirring well. Set mixture aside.

Coat a wok or large nonstick skillet with cooking spray; add oil. Heat at medium-high (375°) until hot. Add carrot, green onions, and peppers; stir-fry 3 minutes. Remove vegetables from wok.

Add chicken to wok; stir-fry 5 minutes. Add marinade and vegetables; cook at medium-high, stirring constantly, until thickened. Serve over rice. Yield: 6 servings.

PER SERVING: 283 CALORIES (8% FROM FAT)
FAT 2.6G (SATURATED FAT 0.5G)
PROTEIN 29.0G CARBOHYDRATE 34.0G
CHOLESTEROL 66MG SODIUM 258MG

CHICKEN AND SNOW PEA STIR-FRY

(pictured on page 82)

Vegetable cooking spray
2 teaspoons vegetable oil, divided
4 (4-ounce) skinned, boned chicken breast
    halves, cut into thin strips
1 clove garlic, minced
¾ cup julienne-sliced sweet red pepper
¾ cup julienne-sliced sweet yellow pepper
6 ounces fresh snow pea pods, trimmed
1 cup canned low-sodium chicken broth,
    undiluted
¼ cup low-sodium soy sauce
1 tablespoon plus 1 teaspoon cornstarch
3 tablespoons dry sherry
1 teaspoon peeled, grated gingerroot
¼ cup sesame seeds, toasted
3 cups cooked rice (cooked without salt or fat)

Coat a wok or large nonstick skillet with cooking spray; add 1 teaspoon oil. Heat at medium-high (375°) until hot. Add chicken and garlic; stir-fry 4 minutes or until chicken is lightly browned. Remove from wok, and drain well on paper towels. Wipe drippings from wok with a paper towel.

Add remaining 1 teaspoon oil to wok, and heat at medium-high until hot. Add peppers to wok; stir-fry 2 minutes or until crisp-tender. Add snow peas; stir-fry 2 minutes. Remove vegetable mixture from wok, and keep warm.

Combine broth and next 4 ingredients; stir well. Add chicken, broth mixture, and sesame seeds to wok; stir-fry 3 minutes or until mixture is thickened and bubbly. Stir in vegetable mixture. Serve over rice. Yield: 4 servings.

PER SERVING: 388 CALORIES (19% FROM FAT)
FAT 8.3G (SATURATED FAT 1.3G)
PROTEIN 26.7G CARBOHYDRATE 46.3G
CHOLESTEROL 49MG SODIUM 472MG

CHINESE CHICKEN STIR-FRY

1 tablespoon dry sherry
1 teaspoon cornstarch
1 egg white
3 (4-ounce) skinned, boned chicken breast
    halves, cut into 1-inch cubes
3 tablespoons low-sodium soy sauce
2 tablespoons water
1 tablespoon sake (rice wine)
1½ teaspoons cornstarch
2 teaspoons sesame oil
Vegetable cooking spray
1 tablespoon vegetable oil, divided
1 (16-ounce) package frozen broccoli, green
    beans, pearl onions, and red peppers,
    thawed
1 (8-ounce) can bamboo shoots, drained
1 (6-ounce) package frozen snow pea pods,
    thawed
3 cups cooked rice (cooked without salt or fat)

Combine first 3 ingredients in a medium bowl; beat with a wire whisk until frothy. Add chicken, stirring to coat. Cover and marinate in refrigerator at least 15 minutes.

Combine soy sauce, water, sake, 1½ teaspoons cornstarch, and sesame oil; stir well, and set aside.

Coat a wok or large nonstick skillet with cooking spray; add 2 teaspoons vegetable oil, and heat at medium-high (375°) until hot. Add chicken, and stir-fry 3 minutes or until lightly browned. Remove chicken from wok. Drain and pat dry with paper towels. Wipe drippings from wok with a paper towel.

Add remaining 1 teaspoon vegetable oil to wok; heat at medium-high until hot. Add mixed vegetables, bamboo shoots, and snow peas; stir-fry 3 to 4 minutes or until crisp-tender. Add soy sauce mixture; stir well.

Return chicken to wok. Cook, stirring constantly, until mixture is thickened and thoroughly heated. Serve chicken mixture over rice. Yield: 6 servings.

PER SERVING: 313 CALORIES (18% FROM FAT)
FAT 6.2G (SATURATED FAT 1.2G)
PROTEIN 20.7G   CARBOHYDRATE 42.2G
CHOLESTEROL 36MG   SODIUM 323MG

CURRY-ALMOND CHICKEN

3 tablespoons low-sodium soy sauce, divided
1½ teaspoons cornstarch, divided
¼ teaspoon salt
1 pound skinned, boned chicken breasts, cut
    into bite-size pieces
¼ cup dry sherry
1 tablespoon curry powder
2 tablespoons rice vinegar
1 teaspoon sugar
1 teaspoon dark sesame oil
1 tablespoon vegetable oil
1 cup coarsely chopped sweet yellow pepper
½ cup coarsely chopped onion
1 teaspoon peeled, minced gingerroot
3 cloves garlic, minced
1 (8-ounce) can sliced bamboo shoots, drained
4 cups cooked rice (cooked without salt or fat)
¼ cup sliced green onions
¼ cup slivered almonds, toasted

Combine 1 tablespoon soy sauce, ½ teaspoon cornstarch, salt, and chicken in a bowl; stir well. Cover and marinate in refrigerator 30 minutes. Combine remaining 2 tablespoons soy sauce, remaining 1 teaspoon cornstarch, sherry, and next 4 ingredients in a small bowl; stir well, and set aside.

Heat vegetable oil in a wok or large nonstick skillet at medium-high (375°) until hot. Add yellow pepper, onion, gingerroot, and garlic; stir-fry 3 minutes. Add chicken mixture; stir-fry 5 minutes or until chicken is done. Add sherry mixture and bamboo shoots; stir-fry 1 minute or until thickened and bubbly. For each serving, spoon 1 cup chicken mixture over 1 cup rice; sprinkle each with 1 tablespoon green onions and 1 tablespoon almonds. Yield: 4 servings.

PER SERVING: 500 CALORIES (20% FROM FAT)
FAT 10.9G (SATURATED FAT 1.6G)
PROTEIN 34.0G   CARBOHYDRATE 61.3G
CHOLESTEROL 66MG   SODIUM 591MG

From front: *Curry-Almond Chicken and Beef and Broccoli with Oyster Sauce (recipe on page 57)*

CURRIED CHICKEN ORIENTAL

1½ tablespoons low-sodium soy sauce
1½ tablespoons dry sherry
1 teaspoon peeled, grated gingerroot
1 teaspoon minced garlic
¼ teaspoon salt
3 (4-ounce) skinned, boned chicken breast
    halves, cut into thin strips
Vegetable cooking spray
1 teaspoon peanut oil
¼ cup water
½ cup thinly sliced carrot
⅓ cup julienne-sliced green pepper
⅓ cup thinly sliced green onions
2 ounces fresh snow pea pods, trimmed
1 cup sliced fresh mushrooms
1 (8-ounce) can pineapple chunks in juice,
    drained
¼ cup unsalted dry roasted peanuts
2 teaspoons curry powder
1½ tablespoons cornstarch
1½ cups canned low-sodium chicken broth
2 cups cooked rice (cooked without salt or fat)

Combine first 5 ingredients in a small bowl; stir well. Add chicken, and toss well. Cover and marinate in refrigerator 4 hours, stirring occasionally.

Coat a wok or large nonstick skillet with cooking spray; add oil. Heat at medium-high (375°) until hot. Add chicken and marinade; stir-fry 3 minutes or until chicken is lightly browned. Remove chicken from wok; pat dry with paper towels. Set aside.

Add water to wok, stirring to deglaze pan. Add carrot; stir-fry 2 minutes. Add green pepper and green onions; stir-fry 2 minutes. Add snow peas and mushrooms; stir-fry 1 minute. Add chicken, pineapple, peanuts, and curry powder; toss well.

Combine cornstarch and broth, stirring until smooth. Add to wok; cook, stirring constantly, 1 to 2 minutes or until mixture is thickened and bubbly. Serve over rice. Yield: 4 servings.

PER SERVING: 328 CALORIES (19% FROM FAT)
FAT 6.8G (SATURATED FAT 1.1G)
PROTEIN 25.6G   CARBOHYDRATE 39.7G
CHOLESTEROL 49MG   SODIUM 387MG

CHICKEN IN TOMATO-VEGETABLE SAUCE

While this hearty dish simmers, prepare a salad and heat bread to round out the meal.

1 tablespoon olive oil
1 cup sliced leeks
2 cloves garlic, minced
4 (4-ounce) skinned, boned chicken breast
    halves, cut diagonally into thin strips
1 teaspoon dried basil
1 teaspoon dried oregano
1 (14½-ounce) can no-salt-added whole
    tomatoes, undrained and chopped
1 medium zucchini, sliced
½ cup canned low-sodium chicken broth,
    undiluted
¼ cup dry white wine
¼ teaspoon salt
¼ cup no-salt-added tomato paste
4 cups cooked long-grain rice (cooked without
    salt or fat)
2 tablespoons freshly grated Parmesan cheese
Fresh basil sprigs (optional)

Heat oil in a wok or large nonstick skillet at medium-high (375°) until hot. Add leeks and garlic; stir-fry 3 minutes or until tender. Add chicken, and stir-fry 5 minutes or until chicken is done. Stir in basil and oregano. Remove chicken from skillet; set aside, and keep warm.

Add tomatoes and next 4 ingredients to wok; bring to a boil. Stir in tomato paste; cover, reduce heat, and simmer 10 minutes.

Add chicken, and cook until thoroughly heated. Serve over rice. Sprinkle evenly with Parmesan cheese. Garnish with basil sprigs, if desired. Yield: 4 servings.

PER SERVING: 449 CALORIES (14% FROM FAT)
FAT 7.1G (SATURATED FAT 2.0G)
PROTEIN 33.7G   CARBOHYDRATE 61.1G
CHOLESTEROL 66MG   SODIUM 365MG

Chicken in Tomato-Vegetable Sauce

Stir-Fry Chicken with Vegetables

STIR-FRY CHICKEN WITH VEGETABLES

If Oriental broth is unavailable, canned chicken broth is a fine substitute.

¼ cup canned Oriental broth, undiluted
1 tablespoon cornstarch
1 tablespoon low-sodium soy sauce
4 (4-ounce) skinned, boned chicken breast
    halves, cut into ½-inch-wide strips
⅓ cup canned Oriental broth, undiluted
¼ cup low-sodium soy sauce
1 tablespoon cornstarch
2 tablespoons dry sherry
1 tablespoon rice vinegar
1 tablespoon chili puree with garlic
2 teaspoons sugar
1 teaspoon dark sesame oil
Vegetable cooking spray
1 tablespoon vegetable oil, divided
2 large carrots, scraped and thinly sliced
1 green pepper, sliced
1 sweet red pepper, sliced
1 onion, cut into thin strips
4 green onions, chopped
1 tablespoon peeled, minced gingerroot
Additional green onions (optional)

Combine first 3 ingredients; add chicken strips, stirring to coat. Cover and marinate in refrigerator 30 minutes.

Combine ⅓ cup broth and next 7 ingredients; set aside.

Remove chicken from marinade, discarding marinade.

Coat a wok or large nonstick skillet with cooking spray; add 1 teaspoon vegetable oil, and heat at medium-high (375°) until hot. Add chicken, and stir-fry 5 minutes or until tender. Remove chicken from wok, and set aside.

Heat remaining 2 teaspoons vegetable oil in wok; add carrot, and stir-fry 2 to 3 minutes. Add green pepper and next 4 ingredients; stir-fry 3 minutes.

Stir in broth mixture; bring to a boil. Boil 1 minute or until thickened. Stir in chicken; garnish with green onions, if desired. Yield: 4 servings.

Note: One pound fresh turkey breast may be substituted for chicken, if desired.

PER SERVING: 305 CALORIES (27% FROM FAT)
FAT 9.0G (SATURATED FAT 2.0G)
PROTEIN 36.7G CARBOHYDRATE 16.0G
CHOLESTEROL 97MG SODIUM 667MG

SESAME CHICKEN WITH SUMMER VEGETABLES

Vegetable cooking spray
1 teaspoon sesame oil
2 (4-ounce) skinned, boned chicken breast
    halves, cut into thin strips
1 cup chopped yellow squash
1 cup sliced zucchini
1 small onion, cut into wedges
½ cup sliced sweet red pepper
3 tablespoons canned low-sodium chicken
    broth, undiluted
2 teaspoons low-sodium soy sauce
2 teaspoons sesame seeds, toasted

Coat a wok or medium nonstick skillet with cooking spray; add oil. Heat at medium-high (375°) until hot. Add chicken, and stir-fry 5 minutes. Remove chicken from wok; set aside, and keep warm. Wipe drippings from wok with a paper towel.

Coat wok with cooking spray. Heat at medium-high until hot. Add yellow squash and zucchini; stir-fry 3 minutes. Stir in onion and red pepper; stir-fry 1 minute. Add chicken, chicken broth, and soy sauce. Cook 3 minutes, stirring frequently. Sprinkle with sesame seeds. Yield: 2 servings.

PER SERVING: 243 CALORIES (21% FROM FAT)
FAT 8.1G (SATURATED FAT 1.6G)
PROTEIN 29.6G CARBOHYDRATE 13.1G
CHOLESTEROL 70MG SODIUM 207MG

CHICKEN-CARAMBOLA STIR-FRY

Carambolas, or star fruit, take the place of pineapple or oranges in this one-dish meal.

4 carambolas (about ¾ pound)
1 pound skinned, boned chicken breasts, cut into ¼-inch-wide strips
¼ cup sherry
2 tablespoons brown sugar
2 tablespoons peeled, minced gingerroot
1 tablespoon low-sodium soy sauce
4 cloves garlic, crushed
3 tablespoons cornstarch
1 teaspoon vegetable oil
1½ cups julienne-sliced sweet red pepper
1 cup vertically sliced onion
2 teaspoons dark sesame oil
¼ teaspoon salt
⅛ teaspoon pepper
4 cups cooked rice (cooked without salt or fat)

Cut 1 carambola in half crosswise, and squeeze 2 tablespoons juice, using a citrus reamer or juicer; set juice aside. Dice carambola halves, and set aside. Slice remaining 3 carambolas crosswise, and set aside.

Combine 2 tablespoons carambola juice, chicken, sherry, brown sugar, gingerroot, soy sauce, and garlic in a bowl; stir well. Cover and marinate in refrigerator 30 minutes.

Drain chicken, reserving marinade. Sprinkle chicken with cornstarch; toss well to coat.

Heat vegetable oil in a wok or large nonstick skillet at medium-high (375°) until hot. Add chicken and carambola; stir-fry 1 minute. Add sweet red pepper and onion, and stir-fry 3 minutes or until chicken is done. Add reserved marinade, sesame oil, salt, and pepper; stir-fry 1 minute. For each serving, spoon 1 cup chicken mixture over 1 cup rice. Yield: 4 servings.

PER SERVING: 483 CALORIES (10% FROM FAT)
FAT 5.6G (SATURATED FAT 1.0G)
PROTEIN 32.1G   CARBOHYDRATE 74.2G
CHOLESTEROL 66MG   SODIUM 486MG

EASY SWEET-AND-SOUR CHICKEN

1 tablespoon vegetable oil
1 pound skinned, boned chicken breasts, cut into 1-inch pieces
1 cup julienne-sliced green pepper
1 cup julienne-sliced carrot
1 clove garlic, minced
¾ cup canned low-sodium chicken broth, undiluted
½ cup low-sodium teriyaki marinade and sauce
1 tablespoon cornstarch
3 tablespoons brown sugar
3 tablespoons white vinegar
2 tablespoons sherry
½ teaspoon ground ginger
1 (8-ounce) can unsweetened pineapple chunks, undrained
5 cups cooked rice (cooked without salt or fat)

Heat oil in a wok or large nonstick skillet at medium-high (375°) until hot. Add chicken; stir-fry 5 minutes or until chicken is browned. Add green pepper, carrot, and garlic, and stir-fry 2 minutes.

Combine broth and next 6 ingredients, stirring well. Add broth mixture and pineapple to wok; bring to a boil, and cook, stirring constantly, 1 minute or until thickened and bubbly. For each serving, spoon 1 cup chicken mixture over 1 cup rice. Yield: 5 servings.

PER SERVING: 440 CALORIES (9% FROM FAT)
FAT 4.5G (SATURATED FAT 0.8G)
PROTEIN 27.0G   CARBOHYDRATE 71.2G
CHOLESTEROL 53MG   SODIUM 490MG

CHICKEN AND SHRIMP FRIED RICE

½ pound unpeeled medium-size fresh shrimp
½ pound skinned, boned chicken breasts, diced
1 teaspoon rice vinegar
1 teaspoon peeled, minced gingerroot
4 cups cooked rice (cooked without salt or fat)
¼ cup low-sodium soy sauce
1 tablespoon plus 2 teaspoons vegetable oil,
    divided
2 cloves garlic, minced
1½ cups finely chopped cabbage
½ cup minced green onions
½ cup frozen English peas, thawed
¼ teaspoon pepper
Pineapple-Cucumber Relish

Peel and devein shrimp. Combine shrimp, chicken, vinegar, and gingerroot. Let stand 10 minutes. Combine rice and soy sauce; stir well. Set aside.

Heat 2 teaspoons oil in a wok or large nonstick skillet at medium-high (375°) until hot. Add shrimp mixture; stir-fry 3 minutes. Remove from wok; set aside.

Heat remaining 1 tablespoon oil in wok at medium-high. Add garlic, and stir-fry 30 seconds. Add next 3 ingredients; stir-fry 4 minutes. Add shrimp mixture, rice mixture, and pepper; stir-fry 3 minutes. Serve with relish. Yield: 6 servings.

PINEAPPLE-CUCUMBER RELISH

1½ cups finely chopped fresh pineapple
2 tablespoons white vinegar
1½ teaspoons sugar
1 teaspoon dried mint flakes
1 medium cucumber, peeled, halved
    lengthwise, and thinly sliced (about 1½ cups)

Combine all ingredients; cover and chill 2 hours. Serve with a slotted spoon. Yield: 6 (½-cup) servings.

PER SERVING: 306 CALORIES (15% FROM FAT)
FAT 5.2G (SATURATED FAT 0.9G)
PROTEIN 19.2G CARBOHYDRATE 45.1G
CHOLESTEROL 65MG SODIUM 410MG

Chicken and Shrimp Fried Rice

CHINESE CHICKEN FRIED RICE

⅔ cup frozen egg substitute, thawed
½ teaspoon dark sesame oil
¼ teaspoon salt
Vegetable cooking spray
2 teaspoons vegetable oil, divided
½ pound skinned, boned chicken breasts, cut into strips
2 teaspoons peeled, minced gingerroot
1 clove garlic, minced
1 cup slivered onion
2 ounces lean, lower-salt cooked ham, cut into very thin strips
3 cups cooked rice (cooked without salt or fat)
1 cup frozen English peas, thawed
2 tablespoons low-sodium soy sauce
2 tablespoons dry sherry
¼ teaspoon salt
1 cup loosely packed thinly sliced romaine lettuce
½ cup sliced green onions

Combine first 3 ingredients in a bowl; stir well, and set aside. Coat a large nonstick skillet with cooking spray; place over medium-high heat until hot. Add egg mixture; cook, stirring constantly, 1½ minutes or until firm but still moist. Remove egg from skillet; set aside.

Wipe skillet with a paper towel. Heat 1 teaspoon vegetable oil in skillet over high heat. Add chicken; stir-fry 2 minutes or until done. Remove from skillet; set aside, and keep warm.

Heat remaining 1 teaspoon vegetable oil in skillet over medium-high heat. Add gingerroot and garlic; stir-fry 10 seconds. Add onion and ham; stir-fry 1 minute. Add rice; stir-fry 2 minutes. Add peas; stir-fry 1 minute. Return egg mixture and chicken to pan. Add soy sauce, sherry, and salt, and cook 30 seconds. Remove from heat; stir in lettuce and green onions. Serve immediately. Yield: 6 (1-cup) servings.

PER SERVING: 241 CALORIES (14% FROM FAT)
FAT 3.7G (SATURATED FAT 0.8G)
PROTEIN 17.4G CARBOHYDRATE 32.8G
CHOLESTEROL 29MG SODIUM 522MG

CURRIED CHICKEN FRIED RICE

1 teaspoon dark sesame oil
½ cup diced onion
1 clove garlic, minced
6 ounces skinned, boned chicken breasts, cut into ½-inch pieces
1 cup frozen English peas, thawed
⅓ cup canned low-sodium chicken broth, undiluted
1 teaspoon curry powder
½ teaspoon ground cumin
1¼ cups cold cooked basmati rice (cooked without salt or fat)
¼ teaspoon salt
⅛ to ¼ teaspoon pepper
Vegetable cooking spray
2 eggs, lightly beaten

Heat oil in a large nonstick skillet over medium-high heat until hot. Add onion and garlic; stir-fry 1 minute. Add chicken; stir-fry 2 to 3 minutes. Add peas, broth, curry powder, and cumin; bring to a boil. Reduce heat, and simmer 2 minutes. Stir in rice, salt, and pepper; cook until thoroughly heated. Spoon mixture into a medium bowl; set aside, and keep warm. Wipe skillet with a paper towel.

Coat skillet with cooking spray, and place over medium heat until hot. Add eggs; tilt skillet so eggs cover bottom. Cook 2 minutes or until almost set (do not stir); turn eggs, and cook 1 additional minute or until set. Remove eggs from skillet, and chop. Add chopped eggs to rice mixture, and stir well. Yield: 2 (1½-cup) servings.

PER SERVING: 418 CALORIES (21% FROM FAT)
FAT 9.9G (SATURATED FAT 2.3G)
PROTEIN 33.7G CARBOHYDRATE 46.9G
CHOLESTEROL 270MG SODIUM 510MG

PENNE WITH CHICKEN, PEAS, AND ASPARAGUS

2½ cups penne (short tubular pasta), uncooked
½ cup canned low-sodium chicken broth, undiluted
1 cup frozen English peas, thawed and divided
1 tablespoon olive oil
1 clove garlic, minced
1½ cups (½-inch) diagonally sliced asparagus
¾ pound skinned, boned chicken breasts, cut into ½-inch pieces
½ teaspoon salt
¼ cup grated Romano or Parmesan cheese
½ teaspoon pepper

Cook pasta according to package directions, omitting salt and fat. Drain and set aside.

Place broth and ½ cup peas in container of an electric blender or food processor; cover and process until smooth. Set aside.

Heat oil in a wok or large nonstick skillet at medium-high (375°) until hot. Add garlic; stir-fry 30 seconds. Add asparagus and chicken; stir-fry 4 minutes or until chicken is done. Add pea puree, remaining ½ cup peas, and salt; stir well. Stir in pasta; bring to a boil. Cook 2 minutes or until mixture thickens, stirring constantly. Remove from heat. Add cheese and pepper; toss well. Yield: 4 (1½-cup) servings.

PER SERVING: 408 CALORIES (17% FROM FAT)
FAT 7.6G (SATURATED FAT 2.1G)
PROTEIN 32.2G   CARBOHYDRATE 48.9G
CHOLESTEROL 57MG   SODIUM 487MG

PESTO AND CHICKEN

4 (4-ounce) skinned, boned chicken breast halves
6 ounces penne (short tubular pasta), uncooked
1 cup firmly packed fresh spinach
2 tablespoons grated Parmesan cheese
1 tablespoon chopped fresh basil
1 tablespoon pine nuts, toasted
½ teaspoon garlic powder
¼ teaspoon dried crushed red pepper
½ cup plain nonfat yogurt
Vegetable cooking spray

Slice chicken diagonally across grain into ¼-inch-wide strips, and set aside.

Cook pasta according to package directions, omitting salt and fat. Drain; set aside, and keep warm.

Combine spinach, Parmesan cheese, basil, pine nuts, garlic powder, and crushed red pepper in container of an electric blender or food processor. Cover and process until smooth. Spoon mixture into a small bowl, and stir in yogurt. Set aside.

Coat a wok or large nonstick skillet with cooking spray; heat at medium-high (375°) until hot. Add chicken, and stir-fry until browned; stir in reserved spinach mixture. Cover, reduce heat, and simmer 5 minutes or until mixture is thoroughly heated and chicken is tender (do not boil).

Add reserved pasta to wok. Toss gently to combine. Serve immediately. Yield: 6 servings.

PER SERVING: 226 CALORIES (16% FROM FAT)
FAT 4.0G (SATURATED FAT 1.0G)
PROTEIN 24.1G   CARBOHYDRATE 22.6G
CHOLESTEROL 72MG   SODIUM 109MG

FYI

Pine nuts, small cream-colored nuts gathered from several types of pine trees, can be found in the nut section of supermarkets and health-food stores. Because they can easily turn rancid, store them in the freezer (up to nine months).

SAGE CHICKEN AND PASTA

Olive oil-flavored vegetable cooking spray
3 (4-ounce) skinned, boned chicken breast
    halves, cut into thin strips
1 medium-size purple onion, thinly sliced
1 medium carrot, scraped and thinly sliced
1 clove garlic, minced
¼ cup water
2 tablespoons dry white wine
6 ounces spaghetti, uncooked
1 tablespoon reduced-calorie margarine
3 plum tomatoes, seeded and chopped
¼ cup sliced ripe olives
¼ cup chopped fresh parsley
1 tablespoon minced fresh sage
¼ cup freshly grated Parmesan cheese

Coat a wok or large nonstick skillet with cooking spray; heat at medium-high (375°) until hot. Add chicken, onion, carrot, and garlic; stir-fry 4 minutes or until chicken is lightly browned. Add water and wine; reduce heat to medium (350°), and simmer, uncovered, 5 minutes. Remove chicken mixture from heat; set aside.

Cook pasta according to package directions, omitting salt and fat. Drain well. Place pasta in a large serving bowl; add margarine, and toss until margarine melts. Add reserved chicken mixture, tomato, olives, parsley, and sage; toss gently. Sprinkle with Parmesan cheese. Yield: 6 (1-cup) servings.

PER SERVING: 221 CALORIES (18% FROM FAT)
FAT 4.5G (SATURATED FAT 1.3G)
PROTEIN 19.1G CARBOHYDRATE 25.7G
CHOLESTEROL 36MG SODIUM 191MG

SPAGHETTI WITH CHICKEN, WILD MUSHROOMS, AND SAGE

1 ounce dried porcini mushrooms
1 cup hot water
4 ounces spaghetti, uncooked
1 tablespoon olive oil
1 cup coarsely chopped onion
2 teaspoons rubbed sage
2 small cloves garlic, minced
¾ pound skinned, boned chicken breasts, cut
    into ¼-inch-wide strips
¼ teaspoon salt
⅛ teaspoon pepper
Chopped fresh parsley (optional)

Soak porcini mushrooms in hot water 20 minutes; drain, reserving ½ cup liquid.

Cook spaghetti according to package directions, omitting salt and fat. Drain and set aside.

Heat oil in a wok or large nonstick skillet at medium-high (375°) until hot. Add onion, sage, and garlic; stir-fry 2 minutes. Add chicken; stir-fry 3 minutes. Add mushrooms, reserved mushroom liquid, salt, and pepper. Reduce heat to medium (350°); cook, uncovered, 2 minutes or until chicken is done. Add cooked spaghetti; toss well. Sprinkle with chopped parsley, if desired. Yield: 4 (1-cup) servings.

PER SERVING: 279 CALORIES (17% FROM FAT)
FAT 5.2G (SATURATED FAT 0.9G)
PROTEIN 24.7G CARBOHYDRATE 31.5G
CHOLESTEROL 49MG SODIUM 206MG

Mushroom Magic

Porcini mushrooms, or cèpes, are wild, brown, woodsy-tasting mushrooms. They are more readily available in the dried form but can be found fresh in the produce section of large supermarkets. Dried mushrooms must be soaked in hot water to soften them before they are used.

Store fresh porcini mushrooms in the refrigerator in a paper bag or kitchen towel. Dried mushrooms should be stored in an airtight container in a cool, dark place.

Moroccan Chicken and Orzo

MOROCCAN CHICKEN AND ORZO

1 teaspoon paprika
½ teaspoon ground cumin
¼ teaspoon salt
¼ teaspoon threads of saffron
⅛ teaspoon ground cinnamon
1 clove garlic, minced
4 (4-ounce) skinned, boned chicken breast
    halves, cut into 1-inch pieces
Vegetable cooking spray
2 teaspoons vegetable oil
1¼ cups chopped onion
1 cup canned low-sodium chicken broth,
    undiluted
¼ cup golden raisins
1 cup orzo, uncooked
¼ cup chopped fresh cilantro
Fresh cilantro leaves (optional)

Combine first 6 ingredients in a medium bowl. Add chicken, tossing to coat. Set aside.

Coat a wok or nonstick skillet with cooking spray; add oil. Heat at medium-high (375°) until hot. Add onion; stir-fry 4 minutes. Add chicken mixture, and stir-fry 6 minutes or until chicken is browned. Add broth and raisins; reduce heat to medium (350°), and cook 5 minutes.

Cook orzo according to package directions, omitting salt and fat; drain. Add orzo to wok, stirring until heated. Spoon mixture into individual serving bowls. Sprinkle with chopped cilantro. Garnish with cilantro leaves, if desired. Yield: 5 (1-cup) servings.

PER SERVING: 327 CALORIES (12% FROM FAT)
FAT 4.3G (SATURATED FAT 0.8G)
PROTEIN 27.8G   CARBOHYDRATE 43.4G
CHOLESTEROL 53MG   SODIUM 199MG

CHICKEN AND VEGETABLE LO MEIN

Bok choy is a Chinese vegetable with white stalks and dark green leaves. Store it in an airtight container in the refrigerator up to four days.

6 ounces vermicelli, uncooked
2 (4-ounce) skinned, boned chicken breast halves, cut into thin strips
½ teaspoon dried crushed red pepper
2 cloves garlic, minced
Vegetable cooking spray
2 teaspoons dark sesame oil, divided
3 cups sliced bok choy
¾ cup canned low-sodium chicken broth, undiluted
2 tablespoons low-sodium soy sauce
1 tablespoon oyster sauce
½ cup coarsely shredded carrot
⅓ cup diagonally sliced green onions
2 teaspoons sesame seeds, toasted

Cook pasta according to package directions, omitting salt and fat; drain and set aside.

Combine chicken, crushed red pepper, and garlic, tossing well.

Coat a wok or large nonstick skillet with cooking spray; add 1 teaspoon sesame oil. Heat at medium-high (375°) until hot. Add chicken mixture; stir-fry 2 minutes. Add bok choy; stir-fry 2 minutes. Add chicken broth, soy sauce, and oyster sauce to wok; stir-fry 1 minute. Add carrot and green onions; stir-fry 1 minute.

Add cooked pasta and remaining 1 teaspoon sesame oil to wok; toss gently until thoroughly heated. Sprinkle with sesame seeds. Serve immediately. Yield: 4 (1¼-cup) servings.

PER SERVING: 282 CALORIES (17% FROM FAT)
FAT 5.2G (SATURATED FAT 0.8G)
PROTEIN 20.8G CARBOHYDRATE 36.7G
CHOLESTEROL 33MG SODIUM 439MG

PEKING CHICKEN

Peking duck is simplified and made healthier by using chicken. The customary Mandarin pancakes have been replaced with flour tortillas.

1 cup hoisin sauce
¼ cup low-sodium soy sauce
¼ cup rice vinegar
¼ cup honey
1 tablespoon peeled, grated gingerroot
4 cloves garlic, minced
2 pounds skinned, boned chicken breasts
Vegetable cooking spray
1 tablespoon dark sesame oil, divided
8 (8-inch) flour tortillas
1 cup sliced green onions

Combine first 6 ingredients in a medium bowl; stir well. Reserve 1 cup hoisin sauce mixture; set aside. Cut chicken diagonally across grain into thin slices. Add chicken to remaining sauce mixture in bowl, and stir well. Cover and marinate in refrigerator up to 8 hours, stirring occasionally. Remove chicken from bowl; discard marinade.

Coat a wok or large nonstick skillet with cooking spray; add 1½ teaspoons oil, and heat at medium-high (375°) until hot. Add half of chicken; stir-fry 5 minutes or until done. Remove chicken from wok, and set aside. Repeat procedure with remaining 1½ teaspoons oil and chicken.

Heat tortillas according to package directions. Spread 2 tablespoons reserved hoisin sauce mixture down the center of each tortilla. Arrange chicken slices and green onions evenly down center of each tortilla; roll up. Yield: 8 servings.

PER SERVING: 393 CALORIES (15% FROM FAT)
FAT 6.6G (SATURATED FAT 1.1G)
PROTEIN 31.8G CARBOHYDRATE 49.7G
CHOLESTEROL 66MG SODIUM 920MG

CHICKEN FAJITAS

4 (4-ounce) skinned, boned chicken breast
    halves, cut crosswise into thin strips
2 teaspoons vegetable oil
1 tablespoon fresh lime juice
1 teaspoon ground cumin
1 (14½-ounce) can no-salt-added whole
    tomatoes, drained and chopped
1 (4-ounce) can chopped green chiles, drained
2 green onions, sliced
3 tablespoons chopped fresh cilantro
¼ teaspoon salt
¼ teaspoon pepper
8 (6-inch) flour tortillas
Vegetable cooking spray
½ cup low-fat sour cream
1 lime, cut into 8 wedges

Place chicken strips in a heavy-duty, zip-top plastic bag. Combine oil, lime juice, and cumin; pour over chicken. Seal bag, and shake until chicken is well coated. Marinate chicken in refrigerator at least 30 minutes, turning bag occasionally.

Combine tomatoes and next 5 ingredients in a small bowl; stir well. Set aside.

Heat tortillas according to package directions; set aside, and keep warm.

Remove chicken from marinade; discard marinade.

Coat a wok or large nonstick skillet with cooking spray; heat at medium-high (375°) until hot. Add chicken, and stir-fry 5 minutes or until done.

Place chicken evenly down centers of tortillas. Top each with 2 tablespoons tomato mixture and 1 tablespoon sour cream; roll up tortillas. Place 2 fajitas on each of 4 individual serving plates; top with remaining tomato mixture. Serve immediately with lime wedges. Yield: 4 servings.

PER SERVING: 434 CALORIES (24% FROM FAT)
FAT 11.4G (SATURATED FAT 3.6G)
PROTEIN 34.3G CARBOHYDRATE 47.7G
CHOLESTEROL 77MG SODIUM 816 MG

TURKEY-VEGETABLE STIR-FRY

1 pound turkey breast cutlets
¼ cup dry sherry
2 tablespoons low-sodium soy sauce
2 tablespoons water
1 teaspoon brown sugar
Vegetable cooking spray
1 tablespoon vegetable oil
1 clove garlic, minced
1 cup fresh broccoli flowerets
1 medium onion, thinly sliced
2 medium carrots, scraped and cut diagonally
    into ½-inch slices
1 cup sliced fresh mushrooms
1 medium-size sweet red pepper, seeded and
    cut into ¼-inch strips
2 teaspoons cornstarch
2 cups cooked brown rice (cooked without salt
    or fat)

Cut turkey across grain into 3- x ½-inch strips; place in a shallow container, and set aside.

Combine sherry, soy sauce, water, and brown sugar; mix well. Pour over turkey, tossing to coat. Cover and marinate in refrigerator 30 minutes.

Coat a wok or large nonstick skillet with cooking spray. Add oil, and heat at medium-high (375°) until hot. Add garlic; stir-fry 1 minute. Drain turkey, reserving marinade. Add turkey strips to wok; stir-fry 2 minutes. Add broccoli, onion, and carrot; stir-fry 2 minutes. Add mushrooms and red pepper; stir-fry 2 minutes.

Add cornstarch to reserved marinade, stirring well. Pour over turkey mixture. Cook, stirring constantly, 2 minutes or until slightly thickened. Serve over rice. Yield: 4 servings.

PER SERVING: 331 CALORIES (18% FROM FAT)
FAT 6.6G (SATURATED FAT 1.4G)
PROTEIN 31.2G CARBOHYDRATE 35.2G
CHOLESTEROL 68MG SODIUM 294MG

TURKEY AND VEGETABLES FOR TWO

Vegetable cooking spray
½ pound turkey breast, cut into 2- x ½-inch strips
1 teaspoon Dijon mustard
½ teaspoon peeled, grated gingerroot
⅛ teaspoon dried thyme
⅛ teaspoon salt
Dash of ground white pepper
1 clove garlic, minced
1½ cups fresh bean sprouts
½ cup coarsely shredded carrot
¼ cup sliced green onions

Coat a wok or large nonstick skillet with cooking spray; heat at medium-high (375°) until hot. Add turkey; stir-fry 5 minutes. Add mustard and next 5 ingredients; stir-fry 30 seconds. Add remaining ingredients; cook, stirring constantly, 1 additional minute. Serve warm. Yield: 2 (1¼-cup) servings.

PER SERVING: 175 CALORIES (12% FROM FAT)
FAT 2.3G (SATURATED FAT 0.6G)
PROTEIN 29.5G   CARBOHYDRATE 8.7G
CHOLESTEROL 68MG   SODIUM 309MG

TOMATO-TURKEY STIR-FRY

1 pound boneless turkey breast slices
½ teaspoon dried rosemary, crushed
¼ teaspoon cracked pepper
¼ cup dry white wine
1 teaspoon cornstarch
Vegetable cooking spray
2 teaspoons peanut oil
1½ cups fresh broccoli flowerets
½ cup chopped onion
2 firm ripe tomatoes, cut into 16 wedges
2 tablespoons pine nuts, toasted

Cut turkey into thin strips. Sprinkle with rosemary and pepper, and set aside. Combine wine and cornstarch; stir well, and set aside.

Coat a wok or large nonstick skillet with cooking spray. Add oil; heat at medium-high (375°) until hot. Add turkey; stir-fry 2 minutes. Add broccoli and onion; stir-fry 2 minutes. Add tomato. Pour reserved wine mixture over vegetable mixture. Cook, stirring constantly, 2 minutes or until slightly thickened and heated. Transfer to a bowl; sprinkle with pine nuts. Yield: 6 servings.

PER SERVING: 147 CALORIES (29% FROM FAT)
FAT 4.8G (SATURATED FAT 1.0G)
PROTEIN 20.0G   CARBOHYDRATE 6.6G
CHOLESTEROL 45MG   SODIUM 61MG

TURKEY PAPRIKASH

2 tablespoons tomato paste
1 (8-ounce) carton plain low-fat yogurt
1 (8-ounce) package medium egg noodles, uncooked
Vegetable cooking spray
2 teaspoons vegetable oil
1 cup slivered onion
2 cloves garlic, minced
1 pound turkey tenderloin, cut into ½-inch cubes
⅓ cup canned no-salt-added chicken broth, undiluted
2 tablespoons Hungarian sweet paprika
½ teaspoon salt
¼ teaspoon pepper

Combine tomato paste and yogurt; stir well, and set aside.

Cook egg noodles according to package directions, omitting salt and fat. Drain and set aside.

Coat a wok or large nonstick skillet with cooking spray; add oil, and heat at medium-high (375°) until hot. Add onion, garlic, and turkey; stir-fry 3 to 4 minutes or until turkey is no longer pink. Add broth and remaining 3 ingredients; stir well. Cover, reduce heat, and simmer 5 minutes. Remove from heat; let stand 1 minute. Stir in yogurt mixture and egg noodles. Yield: 6 (1-cup) servings.

PER SERVING: 294 CALORIES (16% FROM FAT)
FAT 5.3G (SATURATED FAT 1.4G)
PROTEIN 26.0G   CARBOHYDRATE 34.8G
CHOLESTEROL 84MG   SODIUM 283MG

QUICK TURKEY "FRIED" RICE

1¼ cups water
1½ cups instant brown rice, uncooked
2 tablespoons reduced-calorie margarine
2 cups chopped cooked turkey
½ cup frozen English peas, thawed
½ cup coarsely shredded carrot
¼ cup thinly sliced green onions
¼ cup coarsely chopped green pepper
2 tablespoons low-sodium soy sauce
1 egg, lightly beaten

Bring water to a boil in a saucepan; stir in rice. Cook rice according to package directions, omitting salt and fat. Cover rice, and set aside.

Melt margarine in a large nonstick skillet over medium-high heat. Add turkey, and stir-fry 1 minute. Add peas, carrot, green onions, and green pepper. Stir-fry 3 minutes. Add soy sauce, and reduce heat to medium. Stir in egg, and cook, stirring constantly, 1 minute.

Combine rice and turkey mixture; stir well. Serve warm. Yield: 5 (1-cup) servings.

PER SERVING: 353 CALORIES (19% FROM FAT)
FAT 7.5G (SATURATED FAT 1.2G)
PROTEIN 23.1G   CARBOHYDRATE 46.8G
CHOLESTEROL 82MG   SODIUM 273MG

Quick Turkey "Fried" Rice

Mexican Turkey-Bean Salad

MEXICAN TURKEY-BEAN SALAD

Serve this main dish salad with toasted pita bread rounds and sliced plums as accompaniments.

¼ cup plus 2 tablespoons salsa, divided
¼ cup plus 2 tablespoons white vinegar, divided
Vegetable cooking spray
½ pound freshly ground raw turkey breast
½ teaspoon chili powder
¼ teaspoon dried oregano
⅛ teaspoon pepper
1 (15-ounce) can dark red kidney beans, drained
8 cherry tomatoes, quartered
⅓ cup thinly sliced green onions
⅓ cup chopped sweet yellow pepper
3 cups torn iceberg lettuce
3 cups torn curly endive
1 cup frozen green beans, thawed and drained

Combine 3 tablespoons salsa and 3 tablespoons vinegar in a small jar; cover tightly, and shake vigorously. Set salsa mixture aside.

Coat a wok or large nonstick skillet with cooking spray; heat at medium-high (375°) until hot. Add turkey and next 3 ingredients; stir-fry until turkey is browned. Drain and pat dry with paper towels.

Combine turkey mixture, kidney beans, tomatoes, green onions, and sweet yellow pepper in a large bowl; toss gently. Add remaining 3 tablespoons salsa and remaining 3 tablespoons vinegar; toss gently.

Place iceberg lettuce and curly endive in a large bowl; spoon turkey mixture over lettuce mixture. Top with green beans, and drizzle with reserved salsa mixture. Yield: 5 servings.

PER SERVING: 128 CALORIES (13% FROM FAT)
FAT 1.8G (SATURATED FAT 0.4G)
PROTEIN 14.3G CARBOHYDRATE 14.8G
CHOLESTEROL 23MG SODIUM 256MG

PENNE PASTA WITH SMOKED TURKEY SAUSAGE

1 (8-ounce) carton plain nonfat yogurt
¾ cup evaporated skimmed milk
¼ cup dry white wine
2 tablespoons Dijon mustard
2 tablespoons white wine vinegar
1½ tablespoons coarse-grained mustard
½ teaspoon dried oregano
½ teaspoon dried thyme
½ teaspoon pepper
5 ounces penne (short tubular pasta), uncooked
Olive oil-flavored vegetable cooking spray
1½ cups chopped onion
1½ cups sliced fresh mushrooms
¼ cup plus 2 tablespoons chopped green pepper
1½ tablespoons minced garlic
3 ounces smoked turkey sausage, sliced

Place a colander in a 2-quart glass measure or medium bowl. Line colander with 4 layers of cheesecloth, allowing cheesecloth to extend over edges. Spoon yogurt into colander. Cover loosely with plastic wrap; chill 12 hours.

Combine milk and next 7 ingredients in a bowl. Add ¼ cup yogurt cheese, stirring well; set aside. Reserve remaining yogurt cheese for another use; discard strained liquid.

Cook pasta according to package directions, omitting salt and fat; drain. Set aside, and keep warm.

Coat a wok or large nonstick skillet with cooking spray; heat at medium-high (375°) until hot. Add onion and remaining 4 ingredients; stir-fry until vegetables are tender and sausage is browned.

Add pasta to vegetable mixture. Cook, stirring constantly, until thoroughly heated. Remove from heat. Add yogurt mixture, stirring well. Serve immediately. Yield: 5 (1-cup) servings.

PER SERVING: 246 CALORIES (19% FROM FAT)
FAT 5.2G (SATURATED FAT 1.2G)
PROTEIN 12.1G CARBOHYDRATE 35.5G
CHOLESTEROL 22MG SODIUM 438MG

Oriental Wild Rice (recipe on page 108)

GRAIN & PASTA SIDE DISHES

*T*his collection of recipes features not only traditional stir-fried rice dishes but also stir-fries that call for barley, couscous, and pasta.

Turn to page 107 to find a recipe for Spanish Fried Rice and to page 108 for Oriental Wild Rice. Also on pages 108 and 109 are recipes for barley and couscous, followed by several featuring pasta. Indonesian Pasta (page 112) is an unusual dish for two that's made with fresh asparagus, sweet red pepper, and capellini.

In most of the recipes, the grain or pasta is cooked in a saucepan and then tossed with various combinations of stir-fried vegetables. As with all stir-fries, avoid overcooking the vegetables so that their crisp textures are preserved.

Mexican Black Beans and Rice

MEXICAN BLACK BEANS AND RICE

2 teaspoons olive oil
1 cup chopped onion
½ cup chopped green pepper
2 cups cooked long-grain rice (cooked without
    salt or fat)
½ teaspoon ground cumin
¼ teaspoon ground red pepper
⅛ teaspoon ground coriander
1 (15-ounce) can black beans, rinsed and
    drained
¾ cup chopped tomato

Heat olive oil in a wok or large nonstick skillet at medium-high (375°) until hot. Add onion and green pepper; stir-fry until tender. Stir in rice and next 3 ingredients; stir-fry 3 minutes. Add beans and tomato; stir-fry 3 minutes or until thoroughly heated. Yield: 8 (½-cup) servings.

PER SERVING: 118 CALORIES (11% FROM FAT)
FAT 1.5G (SATURATED FAT 0.2G)
PROTEIN 4.2G CARBOHYDRATE 22.4G
CHOLESTEROL 0MG SODIUM 56MG

SPANISH FRIED RICE

1 tablespoon olive oil, divided
4 cups cooked rice (cooked without salt or fat)
1/8 teaspoon powdered saffron
1/2 cup chopped onion
1/4 cup chopped celery
1/4 cup chopped green pepper
1/4 cup chopped sweet red pepper
2 cloves garlic, crushed
1/4 cup no-salt-added tomato sauce
1 teaspoon chili powder
1/2 teaspoon sugar
1/2 teaspoon salt
Dash of ground red pepper
1 (14 1/2-ounce) can no-salt-added whole
    tomatoes, drained and chopped

Heat 1 1/2 teaspoons oil in a wok or large nonstick skillet at medium (350°) until hot. Add rice and saffron; cook, stirring constantly, 3 minutes. Remove from wok; set aside.

Heat remaining 1 1/2 teaspoons oil in wok at medium-high (375°) until hot. Add onion and next 4 ingredients; stir-fry 2 minutes or until tender. Add tomato sauce and remaining 5 ingredients; cook 2 minutes, stirring frequently. Return rice to wok, and stir-fry until thoroughly heated. Yield: 5 (1-cup) servings.

PER SERVING: 232 CALORIES (12% FROM FAT)
FAT 3.1G (SATURATED FAT 0.4G)
PROTEIN 4.3G CARBOHYDRATE 46.5G
CHOLESTEROL 0MG SODIUM 255MG

EASY SPANISH RICE

Vegetable cooking spray
1 cup uncooked instant rice
1 cup chopped onion
2/3 cup diced green pepper
1/2 teaspoon prepared mustard
1/4 teaspoon pepper
1 (14.5-ounce) can whole tomatoes, undrained
    and chopped
1 (5.5-ounce) can tomato juice

Coat a wok or large nonstick skillet with cooking spray; heat at medium-high (375°) until hot. Add rice, onion, and green pepper; stir-fry 4 to 5 minutes. Add remaining ingredients; reduce heat, and simmer, uncovered, 5 minutes or until liquid is absorbed. Yield: 3 (1-cup) servings.

PER SERVING: 188 CALORIES (3% FROM FAT)
FAT 0.6G (SATURATED FAT 0.1G)
PROTEIN 4.9G CARBOHYDRATE 41.7G
CHOLESTEROL 0MG SODIUM 705MG

VEGETABLE FRIED RICE

*If serving this as a main dish, count on
four to six servings.*

1 egg
1/8 teaspoon salt
1 tablespoon low-sodium soy sauce
1 teaspoon peanut oil
1/2 teaspoon brown sugar
Vegetable cooking spray
1 cup sliced celery
1/2 cup slivered onion
1 cup sliced fresh mushrooms
1 (6-ounce) package smoked tofu, crumbled
2 cloves garlic, crushed
3 cups cooked rice (cooked without salt or fat)
1 cup frozen English peas, thawed

Combine egg and salt, beating with a wire whisk until frothy. Set aside. Combine soy sauce, oil, and sugar. Set aside.

Coat a wok or large nonstick skillet with cooking spray. Heat at medium-high (375°) until hot. Add celery and onion; stir-fry 2 minutes. Add mushrooms, tofu, and garlic; stir-fry 1 minute.

Push vegetable mixture up sides of wok, forming a well in center. Pour egg mixture into well, and stir-fry until set. Add rice, and stir-fry 1 minute. Add soy sauce mixture and peas; stir-fry 2 minutes. Serve immediately. Yield: 12 (1/2-cup) servings.

PER SERVING: 101 CALORIES (9% FROM FAT)
FAT 1.0G (SATURATED FAT 0.4G)
PROTEIN 5.5G CARBOHYDRATE 15.6G
CHOLESTEROL 19MG SODIUM 102MG

ORIENTAL WILD RICE

(pictured on page 104)

2½ cups water
1 cup wild rice, uncooked
Vegetable cooking spray
1 tablespoon dark sesame oil
2 cups fresh broccoli flowerets
1 cup fresh bean sprouts
⅔ cup diagonally sliced carrot
1 small sweet red pepper, seeded and cut into
    1-inch pieces
4 green onions, cut into 1-inch pieces
1 tablespoon sesame seeds
1 teaspoon peeled, minced gingerroot
2 teaspoons low-sodium soy sauce

Combine water and rice in a medium saucepan; bring to a boil. Cover, reduce heat, and simmer 40 minutes or until rice is tender. Drain and set aside.

Coat a wok or large nonstick skillet with cooking spray; add oil. Heat at medium-high (375°) until hot. Add broccoli and remaining 7 ingredients; stir-fry 3 minutes. Cover and steam until crisp-tender. Add rice; stir-fry until thoroughly heated. Serve immediately. Yield: 6 (1-cup) servings.

PER SERVING: 137 CALORIES (19% FROM FAT)
FAT 2.9G (SATURATED FAT 0.4G)
PROTEIN 5.3G CARBOHYDRATE 24.1G
CHOLESTEROL 0MG SODIUM 57MG

BARLEY-VEGETABLE MEDLEY

1¼ cups quick-cooking barley
2 tablespoons reduced-calorie margarine
1 cup diced carrot
½ cup chopped onion
¼ cup finely chopped fresh parsley
2 teaspoons dried oregano
1 teaspoon garlic powder
¼ teaspoon salt
¼ teaspoon pepper
1 cup diced zucchini
¾ cup fresh asparagus tips

Cook barley according to package directions, omitting salt and fat; set aside, and keep warm.

Melt margarine in a large nonstick skillet over medium-high heat. Add carrot and onion; stir-fry until tender. Add parsley and next 4 ingredients; stir well. Add zucchini and asparagus; stir-fry until tender. Stir in barley; cook, stirring constantly, until heated. Yield: 5 (1-cup) servings.

PER SERVING: 202 CALORIES (16% FROM FAT)
FAT 3.6G (SATURATED FAT 0.7G)
PROTEIN 5.6G CARBOHYDRATE 39.4G
CHOLESTEROL 0MG SODIUM 195MG

PARMESAN COUSCOUS

¾ cup water
¼ teaspoon salt
½ cup couscous, uncooked
10 ounces fresh asparagus
2 teaspoons olive oil
½ cup sliced fresh mushrooms
½ cup finely chopped green onions
⅓ cup chopped sweet red pepper
2 tablespoons chopped fresh parsley
2 tablespoons dry white wine
½ teaspoon dried basil
1 clove garlic, minced
⅓ cup freshly grated Parmesan cheese

Combine water and salt in a small saucepan; bring to a boil. Remove from heat. Add couscous; cover and let stand 5 minutes or until couscous is tender and liquid is absorbed.

Snap off tough ends of asparagus. Remove scales from stalks with a knife or vegetable peeler, if desired. Cut asparagus into 1-inch pieces.

Heat oil in a wok or large nonstick skillet at medium-high (375°) until hot. Add asparagus, mushrooms, and next 6 ingredients. Stir-fry 5 to 6 minutes or until vegetables are tender.

Fluff couscous with a fork. Add vegetable mixture and cheese; toss. Yield: 6 (½-cup) servings.

PER SERVING: 108 CALORIES (28% FROM FAT)
FAT 3.3G (SATURATED FAT 1.3G)
PROTEIN 5.4G CARBOHYDRATE 14.9G
CHOLESTEROL 4MG SODIUM 203MG

COUSCOUS WITH SUMMER VEGETABLES

Vegetable cooking spray
1 teaspoon olive oil
1¼ cups shredded zucchini
1¼ cups shredded carrot
½ cup chopped onion
1 small sweet red pepper, seeded and cut into
    ¼-inch-wide strips
¼ cup chopped fresh parsley
1 tablespoon lemon juice
¼ teaspoon dried savory
¼ teaspoon dried rosemary, crumbled
¾ cup water
¼ teaspoon salt
½ cup couscous, uncooked

Coat a wok or large nonstick skillet with cooking spray; add oil, and heat at medium-high (375°) until hot. Add zucchini, carrot, onion, and red pepper; stir-fry until crisp-tender. Transfer to a large bowl; stir in parsley, lemon juice, savory, and rosemary. Set aside, and keep warm.

Combine water and salt in a small saucepan, and bring to a boil. Remove from heat. Add couscous; cover and let stand 5 minutes or until couscous is tender and liquid is absorbed. Add to vegetable mixture, and toss. Yield: 8 (½-cup) servings.

PER SERVING: 61 CALORIES (13% FROM FAT)
FAT 0.9G (SATURATED FAT 0.1G)
PROTEIN 2.1G CARBOHYDRATE 12.1G
CHOLESTEROL 0MG SODIUM 83MG

Couscous with Summer Vegetables

Vegetable Couscous

VEGETABLE COUSCOUS

Vegetable cooking spray
2 medium-size yellow squash, diced
1 medium zucchini, diced
8 small fresh mushrooms, sliced
1 small sweet red pepper, seeded and diced
¼ cup plus 1 tablespoon commercial fat-free
    Italian dressing, divided
½ cup plus 2 tablespoons water
¼ teaspoon salt
½ cup couscous, uncooked

Coat a wok or large nonstick skillet with cooking spray, and heat at medium-high (375°) until hot. Add yellow squash, zucchini, mushrooms, and sweet red pepper; stir-fry until crisp-tender.

Combine squash mixture and 3 tablespoons dressing in a large serving bowl; toss well. Set aside, and keep warm.

Combine water, remaining 2 tablespoons dressing, and salt in a small saucepan; bring to a boil. Remove from heat, and stir in couscous. Cover and let stand 5 minutes or until liquid is absorbed. Add couscous to reserved vegetable mixture, and toss. Yield: 8 servings.

PER SERVING: 58 CALORIES (6% FROM FAT)
FAT 0.4G (SATURATED FAT 0.0G)
PROTEIN 2.4G   CARBOHYDRATE 12.2G
CHOLESTEROL 0MG   SODIUM 177MG

CAPELLINI WITH BROCCOLI AND CHEESE

6 ounces capellini (angel hair pasta), uncooked
1 pound fresh broccoli
Vegetable cooking spray
2 teaspoons olive oil
1 cup canned low-sodium chicken broth, undiluted
2 cups peeled, seeded, and chopped tomato
½ cup (2 ounces) goat cheese
2 tablespoons sesame seeds, toasted
¼ teaspoon freshly ground pepper

Prepare capellini according to package directions, omitting salt and fat. Drain; set pasta aside, and keep warm.

Wash and trim broccoli; cut into small flowerets, and cut stems diagonally into 1-inch pieces.

Coat a wok or large nonstick skillet with cooking spray; add oil, and heat at medium-high (375°) until hot. Add broccoli, and stir-fry 2 to 3 minutes or until crisp-tender. Add chicken broth, and bring to a boil; stir in tomato and goat cheese. Reduce heat, and stir until cheese melts. Stir in reserved capellini. Add sesame seeds and pepper; toss gently. Serve immediately. Yield: 8 (1-cup) servings.

PER SERVING: 78 CALORIES (31% FROM FAT)
FAT 2.7G (SATURATED FAT 1.2G)
PROTEIN 3.5G CARBOHYDRATE 10.3G
CHOLESTEROL 4MG SODIUM 21MG

EGGPLANT VERMICELLI

Four ounces of capellini (angel hair pasta) may be substituted for vermicelli. It cooks in about 2 minutes.

4 ounces vermicelli, uncooked
Vegetable cooking spray
1 teaspoon olive oil
1 cup peeled, cubed eggplant
1 cup finely chopped onion
2 cloves garlic, minced
1½ teaspoons dried basil
1½ teaspoons dried oregano
¼ teaspoon dried crushed red pepper
1 small zucchini, thinly sliced
¼ pound fresh mushrooms, sliced
2 large tomatoes, chopped
1 tablespoon plus 2 teaspoons grated Parmesan cheese

Cook vermicelli according to package directions, omitting salt and fat. Drain and set aside.

Coat a wok or large nonstick skillet with cooking spray; add oil, and heat at medium-high (375°) until hot. Add eggplant and next 5 ingredients. Stir-fry until vegetables are tender. Add zucchini, mushrooms, and chopped tomato; stir-fry 2 minutes or until mixture is thoroughly heated. Combine reserved vermicelli and vegetable mixture on a large serving platter; toss gently. Sprinkle with Parmesan cheese. Yield: 6 servings.

PER SERVING: 118 CALORIES (14% FROM FAT)
FAT 1.9G (SATURATED FAT 0.5G)
PROTEIN 4.6G CARBOHYDRATE 21.6G
CHOLESTEROL 1MG SODIUM 34MG

Pasta Pointers

• Use a large Dutch oven or stockpot so the pasta moves freely and cooks evenly.

• Don't add salt or oil to the water. For extra flavor, add low-sodium chicken or beef broth instead.

• Bring the water to a rolling boil, and add the pasta gradually so that the water continues to boil. Once the pasta is added, begin timing. Stir frequently—you can't stir too much.

• Begin checking for doneness after the minimum recommended cooking time. Remove a piece of pasta from the water and bite into it; properly cooked pasta will be firm and tender.

INDONESIAN PASTA

¼ cup canned low-sodium chicken broth,
    undiluted
1 tablespoon plus 1 teaspoon reduced-fat
    creamy peanut butter
1 tablespoon low-sodium soy sauce
2 teaspoons lemon juice
1½ teaspoons minced onion
1 teaspoon seeded, minced serrano chile
    pepper
⅛ teaspoon brown sugar
Dash of ground cumin
¼ pound fresh asparagus spears
Vegetable cooking spray
2 tablespoons julienne-sliced sweet red pepper
3 tablespoons sliced green onions
1 tablespoon chopped fresh parsley
2 ounces capellini (angel hair pasta), uncooked
Asparagus spears (optional)

Combine first 8 ingredients in a saucepan; bring to a boil, stirring constantly. Set aside; keep warm.

Snap off tough ends of asparagus. Remove scales from stalks with a knife or vegetable peeler, if desired. Coat a wok or large nonstick skillet with cooking spray; heat at medium-high (375°) until hot. Add asparagus and red pepper; stir-fry 3 minutes or until tender. Add green onions; stir-fry 30 seconds. Remove from heat; stir in parsley.

Cook pasta according to package directions, omitting salt and fat; drain. Place pasta in a serving bowl. Add peanut sauce and vegetable mixture; toss gently. Serve warm. Garnish with additional asparagus spears, if desired. Yield: 2 servings.

PER SERVING: 191 CALORIES (23% FROM FAT)
FAT 4.9G (SATURATED FAT 0.8G)
PROTEIN 7.8G CARBOHYDRATE 30.2G
CHOLESTEROL 0MG SODIUM 256MG

Indonesian Pasta

JAPANESE NOODLES

1 tablespoon dark sesame oil
3 cups cooked lo mein noodles or vermicelli
   (cooked without salt or fat)
½ cup julienne-sliced green onions
1½ teaspoons peeled, grated gingerroot
2 tablespoons low-sodium soy sauce

Heat oil in a wok or large nonstick skillet at medium-high (375°) until hot. Add noodles, tossing to coat with oil. Add green onions and gingerroot; stir-fry 3 minutes or until green onions are tender. Remove from heat. Add soy sauce, and toss well. Yield: 3 (1-cup) servings.

PER SERVING: 259 CALORIES (19% FROM FAT)
FAT 5.6G (SATURATED FAT 0.7G)
PROTEIN 7.3G   CARBOHYDRATE 42.2G
CHOLESTEROL 0MG   SODIUM 268MG

PASTA AND RED PEPPERS

4½ ounces linguine, uncooked
Vegetable cooking spray
1½ teaspoons reduced-calorie margarine
1 medium-size sweet red pepper, cut into strips
¼ cup sliced green onions
1 large clove garlic, minced
⅓ cup commercial fat-free Italian dressing

Cook linguine according to package directions, omitting salt and fat. Drain and set aside.

Coat a medium nonstick skillet with cooking spray; add margarine. Place over medium-high heat until margarine melts. Add pepper, green onions, and garlic; stir-fry until tender. Stir in Italian dressing; stir-fry until thoroughly heated. Add pasta; cook, tossing gently, just until mixture is thoroughly heated. Yield: 2 (1-cup) servings.

PER SERVING: 293 CALORIES (10% FROM FAT)
FAT 3.4G (SATURATED FAT 0.9G)
PROTEIN 9.1G   CARBOHYDRATE 56.2G
CHOLESTEROL 0MG   SODIUM 467MG

SIESTA PASTA

6 ounces spaghetti, uncooked
Vegetable cooking spray
1 cup fresh broccoli flowerets
1 cup thinly sliced carrot
1 cup sliced zucchini
¼ cup sliced onion
1 small sweet yellow pepper, seeded and cut
   into very thin strips
⅓ cup chopped green pepper
10 cherry tomatoes, halved
2 tablespoons commercial oil-free Italian
   dressing
¼ cup grated Parmesan cheese
1 tablespoon minced fresh parsley
¼ teaspoon sweet red pepper flakes

Cook spaghetti according to package directions, omitting salt and fat. Drain and set aside.

Coat a wok or large nonstick skillet with cooking spray; heat at medium-high (375°) until hot. Add broccoli and next 3 ingredients; stir-fry 4 minutes. Add peppers, and stir-fry 4 minutes. Add spaghetti, tomatoes, and Italian dressing; cook just until heated.

Transfer to a serving bowl. Sprinkle with cheese, parsley, and pepper flakes; toss gently to combine. Serve immediately. Yield: 8 (1-cup) servings.

PER SERVING: 123 CALORIES (13% FROM FAT)
FAT 1.8G (SATURATED FAT 0.8G)
PROTEIN 5.3G   CARBOHYDRATE 22.0G
CHOLESTEROL 3MG   SODIUM 119MG

FYI

Sweet peppers, often referred to as bell peppers, are available in several colors including green, yellow, orange, and red. While sweet yellow and red peppers are certainly delicious and colorful, green peppers may be substituted in almost any recipe.

Fettuccine Primavera

FETTUCCINE PRIMAVERA

½ pound fresh asparagus spears
Vegetable cooking spray
2 tablespoons reduced-calorie margarine
2 cups sliced fresh mushrooms
1 cup small fresh broccoli flowerets
1 cup thinly sliced carrot
½ cup sliced green onions
½ cup medium-size sweet red pepper, cut into
   very thin strips
3 tablespoons chopped fresh basil
2 cloves garlic, minced
½ cup dry white wine
¼ teaspoon salt
¼ teaspoon pepper
3½ cups cooked fettuccine (cooked without
   salt or fat)
3 tablespoons freshly grated Parmesan cheese

Snap off tough ends of asparagus. Remove scales from spears with a knife or vegetable peeler, if desired. Cut asparagus diagonally into ¾-inch pieces.

Coat a large nonstick skillet with cooking spray; add margarine. Place over medium-high heat until margarine melts. Add asparagus, mushrooms, and next 6 ingredients; stir-fry until vegetables are crisp-tender. Add wine, salt, and pepper; cook, stirring constantly, 2 minutes. Add fettuccine and cheese; toss well. Serve immediately. Yield: 7 (1-cup) servings.

PER SERVING: 169 CALORIES (12% FROM FAT)
FAT 2.3G (SATURATED FAT 0.5G)
PROTEIN 6.6G   CARBOHYDRATE 31.4G
CHOLESTEROL 1MG   SODIUM 139MG

SESAME-FARFALLE STIR-FRY

If you wish, substitute mostaccioli (tubular pasta) or fusilli (corkscrew pasta) for farfalle pasta.

2 cups farfalle (bow tie pasta), uncooked
3 tablespoons low-sodium soy sauce
2 teaspoons white wine vinegar
2 teaspoons honey
1 tablespoon dark sesame oil
1 cup julienne-sliced sweet red pepper
3 tablespoons minced green onions
2 teaspoons peeled, minced gingerroot
1 large clove garlic, minced
⅛ teaspoon salt
1 teaspoon sesame seeds, toasted

Cook pasta according to package directions, omitting salt and fat. Drain and set aside.

Combine soy sauce, white wine vinegar, and honey in a small bowl; stir well, and set aside.

Heat oil in a wok or large nonstick skillet at high (400°) until hot. Add sweet red pepper, green onions, gingerroot, and garlic; stir-fry 1 minute. Add pasta, soy sauce mixture, and salt; stir-fry 1 minute. Remove from heat; sprinkle with sesame seeds. Yield: 3 (1-cup) servings.

PER SERVING: 291 CALORIES (19% FROM FAT)
FAT 6.2G (SATURATED FAT 0.9G)
PROTEIN 8.5G   CARBOHYDRATE 48.9G
CHOLESTEROL 0MG   SODIUM 581MG

Kitchen Helper

As soon as you get perishables home, store them in the refrigerator or freezer. Keep most fresh produce in plastic bags to slow the dehydration that refrigeration causes. Onions and potatoes keep best in the pantry.

Spinach Noodles with Vegetables

SPINACH NOODLES WITH VEGETABLES

6 ounces spinach noodles, uncooked
Vegetable cooking spray
1 medium onion, chopped
1 clove garlic, crushed
1 medium-size yellow squash, thinly sliced
1 medium zucchini, thinly sliced
1 cup fresh corn, cut from cob
1 tablespoon chopped fresh parsley
¾ teaspoon dried basil
¾ teaspoon dried oregano
¼ teaspoon salt
¼ teaspoon freshly ground pepper
2 medium tomatoes, peeled and chopped

Cook spinach noodles according to package directions, omitting salt and fat; drain. Transfer to a serving platter, and keep warm.

Coat a wok or large nonstick skillet with cooking spray; heat at medium-high (375°) until hot. Add onion and garlic; stir-fry until crisp-tender. Reduce heat to medium (350°). Add yellow squash and next 7 ingredients; cook, stirring constantly, until tender. Stir in tomato. Serve over noodles. Yield: 10 servings.

PER SERVING: 93 CALORIES (10% FROM FAT)
FAT 1.1G (SATURATED FAT 0.2G)
PROTEIN 3.7G   CARBOHYDRATE 18.5G
CHOLESTEROL 0MG   SODIUM 78MG

MUSHROOM-PASTA TOSS

Butter-flavored vegetable cooking spray
1 tablespoon reduced-calorie margarine
1¼ cups sliced fresh mushrooms
3 ounces fresh shiitake mushrooms, sliced
3 ounces fresh crimini mushrooms, sliced
2 teaspoons minced garlic
½ cup chopped fresh parsley
½ cup canned no-salt-added beef broth,
    undiluted
1 tablespoon no-salt-added tomato paste
2 teaspoons chopped fresh marjoram
¼ teaspoon salt
8 ounces rotini (corkscrew pasta), uncooked
1 ounce prosciutto, chopped

Coat a large nonstick skillet with cooking spray; add margarine, and place over medium-high heat until melted. Add mushrooms and garlic; stir-fry 3 minutes or until tender. Stir in parsley and next 4 ingredients; cook, stirring constantly, 1 to 2 minutes or until thoroughly heated. Remove from heat, and keep warm.

Cook pasta according to package directions, omitting salt and fat; drain well. Place pasta in a serving bowl. Add mushroom mixture and chopped prosciutto; toss gently. Serve immediately. Yield: 10 (½-cup) servings.

PER SERVING: 108 CALORIES (13% FROM FAT)
FAT 1.6G (SATURATED FAT 0.3G)
PROTEIN 4.4G   CARBOHYDRATE 19.3G
CHOLESTEROL 2MG   SODIUM 117MG

RATATOUILLE PASTA

1½ cups coarsely chopped tomato
¼ cup chopped fresh basil
2 tablespoons balsamic vinegar
½ teaspoon freshly ground pepper
¼ teaspoon salt
6 ounces radiatore (short, fat rippled pasta),
    uncooked
Vegetable cooking spray
1 tablespoon olive oil
2½ cups coarsely chopped zucchini
4 cups coarsely chopped eggplant
2 teaspoons minced garlic
¼ cup freshly grated Parmesan cheese

Combine first 5 ingredients, stirring well. Cover and let stand 2 hours, stirring occasionally.

Cook pasta according to package directions, omitting salt and fat; drain well. Set pasta aside, and keep warm.

Coat a wok or large nonstick skillet with cooking spray; add oil. Heat at medium-high (375°) until hot. Add zucchini, and stir-fry 3 minutes. Add eggplant and garlic; stir-fry 4 minutes or until vegetables are tender. Add tomato mixture and pasta to vegetable mixture. Cook, stirring constantly, until mixture is thoroughly heated. Add cheese, and toss well. Serve warm. Yield: 6 (1-cup) servings.

PER SERVING: 196 CALORIES (26% FROM FAT)
FAT 5.6G (SATURATED FAT 2.0G)
PROTEIN 8.7G   CARBOHYDRATE 28.9G
CHOLESTEROL 6MG   SODIUM 259MG

Focus on Fitness

Strength training exercises (such as lifting weights) can prevent and even reverse the natural breakdown of muscle mass that comes with age. Such exercises also build bone strength and help aging women and men battle osteoporosis and joint injuries. What's more, exercise promotes loss of body fat, boosts self-confidence, and reduces the risk of heart disease, cancer, and diabetes.

Don't think it's too late to start. Even if you're already up in years, you'll feel better, get stronger, and reduce your health risks if you start moving now. It doesn't have to be a rigorous routine; even moderate exercise such as walking or gardening is beneficial.

Hot and Spicy Vegetables (recipe on page 139)

VEGETABLE VARIETY

What's a stir-fry without vegetables? They add brilliant color, fresh flavor, and crunchy texture to almost any type of meat, fish, or poultry stir-fry. But vegetable stir-fries can stand alone as delicious side dishes, too.

These recipes range from fresh asparagus dishes to Zucchini Italienne (page 139) with three vegetable medleys completing the chapter.

All of the stir-fries, like others in this book, are trimmed of excess fat through the use of nonstick cookware and vegetable cooking spray. Reduced amounts of oil keep fat and calories to a minimum.

As with all stir-fries, be sure to wash, trim, and slice the vegetables before heating the wok. (See page 10 for other helpful stir-fry tips.)

GINGERED ASPARAGUS

1 pound fresh asparagus spears
Vegetable cooking spray
1 teaspoon peeled, minced gingerroot
2 tablespoons low-sodium soy sauce
2 teaspoons sesame seeds, toasted
Dash of pepper
½ teaspoon grated orange rind

Snap off tough ends of asparagus. Remove scales from stalks with a knife or vegetable peeler, if desired. Cut spears into 2-inch pieces.

Coat a wok or large nonstick skillet with cooking spray. Heat at medium-high (375°) until hot. Add asparagus and gingerroot; stir-fry 2 minutes. Add soy sauce, sesame seeds, and pepper; toss well. Sprinkle with orange rind. Yield: 4 servings.

PER SERVING: 32 CALORIES (31% FROM FAT)
FAT 1.1G (SATURATED FAT 0.1G)
PROTEIN 2.6G   CARBOHYDRATE 4.6G
CHOLESTEROL 0MG   SODIUM 244MG

ASPARAGUS STIR-FRY

⅓ cup canned low-sodium chicken broth
2 teaspoons cornstarch
½ teaspoon grated lemon rind
2 tablespoons dry sherry
1 tablespoon lemon juice
1 tablespoon low-sodium soy sauce
½ teaspoon dark sesame oil
¼ teaspoon salt
⅛ teaspoon pepper
1 pound fresh asparagus spears
Vegetable cooking spray
1 teaspoon vegetable oil
2 teaspoons peeled, minced gingerroot
1 large clove garlic, minced
2 tablespoons water
½ cup julienne-sliced sweet red pepper
½ cup sliced water chestnuts, drained
3 green onions, sliced

Combine first 3 ingredients in a small bowl; stir well. Stir in sherry and next 5 ingredients. Set aside.

Snap off tough ends of asparagus. Remove scales with a knife or vegetable peeler, if desired. Cut asparagus diagonally into 2-inch pieces.

Coat a wok or large nonstick skillet with cooking spray; add vegetable oil, and heat at medium-high (375°) until hot. Add gingerroot and garlic; stir-fry 10 seconds. Add asparagus; stir-fry 2 minutes. Add water, cooking until water evaporates. Add red pepper and water chestnuts; stir-fry 1 minute.

Add chicken broth mixture and green onions to wok; cook, stirring constantly, 1 minute or until thickened. Yield: 4 (¾-cup) servings.

PER SERVING: 74 CALORIES (28% FROM FAT)
FAT 2.3G (SATURATED FAT 0.3G)
PROTEIN 2.4G   CARBOHYDRATE 12.0G
CHOLESTEROL 0MG   SODIUM 257MG

SWEET-AND-SOUR APPLES AND CABBAGE

1 medium Granny Smith apple, cored and sliced
2 tablespoons lemon juice
Vegetable cooking spray
1 small onion, sliced and separated into rings
5 cups shredded red cabbage
¼ cup unsweetened white grape juice
2 tablespoons dry white wine
2 tablespoons balsamic vinegar
¼ teaspoon salt
⅛ teaspoon pepper

Combine sliced apple and lemon juice in a small bowl; toss gently, and set aside.

Coat a wok or large nonstick skillet with cooking spray; heat at medium-high (375°) until hot. Add onion; stir-fry until tender. Add cabbage; stir-fry 3 minutes or until crisp-tender. Add reserved apple mixture, grape juice, and remaining ingredients; stir gently. Cook 1 minute or until thoroughly heated. Yield: 10 (½-cup) servings.

PER SERVING: 28 CALORIES (6% FROM FAT)
FAT 0.2G (SATURATED FAT 0.0G)
PROTEIN 0.7G   CARBOHYDRATE 6.5G
CHOLESTEROL 0MG   SODIUM 63MG

Sweet-and-Sour Apples and Cabbage

Broccoli-Sweet Potato Stir-Fry

VEGETABLES JULIENNE

1 (16-ounce) can whole beets, drained
Vegetable cooking spray
½ teaspoon vegetable oil
1 cup julienne-sliced carrot
1 cup julienne-sliced parsnip
4 green onions, cut into ½-inch pieces
¼ teaspoon dried thyme
⅛ teaspoon salt
Dash of pepper

Cut beets into very thin strips; set aside 1 cup. Reserve remaining beets for another use.

Coat a wok or large nonstick skillet with cooking spray; add oil. Heat at medium-high (375°) until hot. Add carrot and remaining 5 ingredients; stir-fry 3 minutes or until vegetables are crisp-tender. Add 1 cup beets; stir gently. Cook until thoroughly heated, stirring gently. Yield: 6 (½-cup) servings.

PER SERVING: 34 CALORIES (13% FROM FAT)
FAT 0.5G (SATURATED FAT 0.1G)
PROTEIN 0.7G CARBOHYDRATE 7.1G
CHOLESTEROL 0MG SODIUM 124MG

BROCCOLI-SWEET POTATO STIR-FRY

2 medium-size sweet potatoes
Vegetable cooking spray
1 tablespoon sesame oil
1 clove garlic, minced
1 cup sliced fresh broccoli stems (¼ inch thick)
½ cup sliced green onions, cut into 1-inch pieces
¼ cup sliced sweet red pepper
1 tablespoon low-sodium soy sauce
1½ teaspoons unsweetened orange juice
⅛ teaspoon ground red pepper

Peel sweet potatoes; cut into ¼-inch-thick slices. Coat a wok or large nonstick skillet with cooking spray. Add oil, and heat at medium-high (375°) until hot. Add sweet potatoes and garlic; stir-fry 4

minutes. Add broccoli, green onions, and sweet red pepper slices; stir-fry 3 minutes or until vegetables are crisp-tender.

Combine soy sauce, orange juice, and ground red pepper. Add to vegetables, and cook, stirring constantly, until thoroughly heated. Yield: 8 (½-cup) servings.

PER SERVING: 102 CALORIES (19% FROM FAT)
FAT 2.1G (SATURATED FAT 0.3G)
PROTEIN 1.9G CARBOHYDRATE 19.8G
CHOLESTEROL 0MG SODIUM 75MG

BROCCOLI-TOMATO STIR-FRY

¼ cup sun-dried tomatoes
½ cup boiling water
Vegetable cooking spray
1 teaspoon olive oil
6½ cups chopped fresh broccoli
1 small onion, cut into wedges
2 cloves garlic, minced
¼ cup plus 2 tablespoons water
1 teaspoon cornstarch
1 teaspoon dried oregano
1 ounce crumbled feta cheese

Combine tomatoes and boiling water in a small bowl; let stand 5 minutes. Drain well, and thinly slice tomatoes. Set aside.

Coat a wok or large nonstick skillet with cooking spray; add oil, and heat at medium-high (375°) until hot. Add broccoli, onion, and garlic; stir-fry 4 to 5 minutes or until vegetables are crisp-tender.

Combine ¼ cup plus 2 tablespoons water, cornstarch, and oregano; add to vegetable mixture, and stir-fry 30 seconds. Add sliced tomato; stir-fry until mixture is thoroughly heated. Transfer to a serving bowl, and sprinkle with cheese. Yield: 5 (1-cup) servings.

PER SERVING: 75 CALORIES (32% FROM FAT)
FAT 2.7G (SATURATED FAT 1.1G)
PROTEIN 4.5G CARBOHYDRATE 10.7G
CHOLESTEROL 5MG SODIUM 149MG

SESAME BROCCOLI STIR-FRY

1 tablespoon brown sugar
3 tablespoons low-sodium soy sauce
3 tablespoons canned no-salt-added beef broth
1½ tablespoons red wine vinegar
1½ teaspoons cornstarch
1 teaspoon peeled, minced gingerroot
4 drops of hot sauce
Vegetable cooking spray
2 teaspoons dark sesame oil
8 cups chopped fresh broccoli
1 large sweet red pepper, cut into thin strips
1 medium onion, cut into wedges
2 cloves garlic, minced
¼ cup sliced water chestnuts
1 tablespoon sesame seeds, toasted

Combine brown sugar and next 6 ingredients in a small bowl, stirring well; set aside.

Coat a wok or large nonstick skillet with cooking spray; add oil. Heat at medium-high (375°) until hot. Add broccoli and next 3 ingredients; stir-fry 4 to 5 minutes or until vegetables are crisp-tender.

Add brown sugar mixture to vegetable mixture. Cook, stirring constantly, until thickened. Add water chestnuts and sesame seeds. Cook, stirring constantly, until heated. Yield: 6 (1-cup) servings.

PER SERVING: 94 CALORIES (29% FROM FAT)
FAT 3.0G (SATURATED FAT 0.4G)
PROTEIN 4.8G   CARBOHYDRATE 14.2G
CHOLESTEROL 0MG   SODIUM 238MG

FARM STAND STIR-FRY

2 large ears fresh white corn
2 teaspoons olive oil
3 cups (2-inch) sliced green beans
½ cup vertically sliced onion
½ teaspoon salt
⅛ teaspoon pepper
2½ cups chopped seeded tomato
1 tablespoon chopped fresh basil
2 teaspoons white wine vinegar

Cut whole kernels from ears of corn; set corn aside, and discard cobs.

Heat oil in a wok or large nonstick skillet at medium-high (375°) until hot. Add green beans and onion; stir-fry 5 minutes or until crisp-tender. Add corn, salt, and pepper; cook at medium (350°) for 5 minutes, stirring occasionally. Remove from heat; stir in tomato, basil, and vinegar. Yield: 5 (1-cup) servings.

PER SERVING: 111 CALORIES (23% FROM FAT)
FAT 2.8G (SATURATED FAT 0.4G)
PROTEIN 3.6G   CARBOHYDRATE 21.7G
CHOLESTEROL 0MG   SODIUM 255MG

HERBED CORN, ZUCCHINI, AND TOMATO

Bursting with garden-fresh flavor, this stir-fry goes great with burgers, steaks, or grilled chicken.

1½ tablespoons reduced-calorie margarine
2 cups fresh corn cut from cob (about 3 ears)
1 medium zucchini, trimmed and thinly sliced
½ cup sliced green onions
¼ cup chopped green pepper
1 cup peeled, chopped tomato
2 teaspoons chopped fresh basil
2 teaspoons chopped fresh oregano
1 teaspoon sugar
¼ teaspoon salt
¼ teaspoon salt-free lemon-pepper seasoning

Melt margarine in a large nonstick skillet over medium-high heat. Add corn and next 3 ingredients; stir-fry 5 minutes or until crisp-tender.

Add tomato and remaining ingredients. Reduce heat to medium, and cook until thoroughly heated, stirring frequently. Yield: 8 (½-cup) servings.

PER SERVING: 60 CALORIES (30% FROM FAT)
FAT 2.0G (SATURATED FAT 0.3G)
PROTEIN 1.9G   CARBOHYDRATE 10.8G
CHOLESTEROL 0MG   SODIUM 104MG

Herbed Corn, Zucchini, and Tomato

Southwestern Jicama, Corn, and Peppers

SOUTHWESTERN JICAMA, CORN, AND PEPPERS

For a novel serving container, blanch sweet pepper halves and fill with corn mixture.

Vegetable cooking spray
1 teaspoon olive oil
2½ cups peeled, finely chopped jicama (about 1 pound)
1½ cups finely chopped green pepper
1 cup frozen whole kernel corn, thawed
½ cup finely chopped onion
½ teaspoon ground cumin
¼ teaspoon salt
¼ teaspoon pepper
2 cloves garlic, minced
½ cup minced fresh cilantro
1 tablespoon capers
Fresh cilantro sprigs (optional)

Coat a wok or large nonstick skillet with cooking spray; add oil. Heat at medium-high (375°) until hot. Add jicama and next 7 ingredients; stir-fry 5 minutes or until vegetables are crisp-tender. Add minced cilantro and capers; stir well. Transfer to a serving bowl, and garnish with cilantro, if desired. Serve immediately. Yield: 4 (¾-cup) servings.

PER SERVING: 100 CALORIES (18% FROM FAT)
FAT 2.0G (SATURATED FAT 0.3G)
PROTEIN 2.7G CARBOHYDRATE 20.1G
CHOLESTEROL 0MG SODIUM 380MG

CORN, ROASTED RED PEPPER, AND ONIONS

1 large sweet red pepper (about ½ pound)
2 teaspoons olive oil
1½ cups chopped onion
2 (10-ounce) packages frozen whole kernel corn, thawed and drained
¼ teaspoon salt
⅛ teaspoon pepper
⅛ teaspoon dried crushed red pepper

Cut sweet red pepper in half lengthwise; discard seeds and membranes. Place pepper, skin side up, on a baking sheet; flatten with palm of hand. Broil 3 inches from heat (with electric oven door partially opened) 10 minutes or until blackened and charred. Place in ice water, and chill 5 minutes. Drain; discard skins. Dice pepper, and set aside.

Heat oil in a wok or large nonstick skillet at medium-high (375°) until hot. Add onion, and stir-fry 3 minutes or until tender. Add roasted pepper, corn, and remaining ingredients; cook at medium (350°) for 4 minutes or until thoroughly heated, stirring frequently. Yield: 8 (½-cup) servings.

PER SERVING: 87 CALORIES (19% FROM FAT)
FAT 1.8G (SATURATED FAT 0.3G)
PROTEIN 2.6G CARBOHYDRATE 18.0G
CHOLESTEROL 0MG SODIUM 77MG

HERBED MUSHROOMS AND LEEKS

Vegetable cooking spray
2 teaspoons reduced-calorie margarine
2 cups sliced leeks
1 pound fresh mushrooms, quartered
2 tablespoons low-sodium soy sauce
½ teaspoon dried oregano
¼ teaspoon pepper

Coat a large nonstick skillet with cooking spray; add margarine, and place over medium-high heat until margarine melts. Add leeks; stir-fry 3 minutes. Add mushrooms and remaining ingredients; stir-fry 4 minutes or until mushrooms are tender. Yield: 7 (½-cup) servings.

PER SERVING: 42 CALORIES (24% FROM FAT)
FAT 1.1G (SATURATED FAT 0.2G)
PROTEIN 1.8G CARBOHYDRATE 7.1G
CHOLESTEROL 0MG SODIUM 130MG

MUSHROOM TRIO

Olive oil-flavored vegetable cooking spray
1 teaspoon olive oil
8 ounces fresh crimini mushrooms, stems
     removed
8 ounces portobello mushrooms, stems
     removed
4 ounces small fresh shiitake mushrooms,
     stems removed
1 large clove garlic, minced
⅓ cup dry white wine
2 teaspoons chopped fresh thyme
¼ teaspoon salt
⅛ teaspoon pepper

Coat a wok or large nonstick skillet with cooking spray; add oil. Heat at medium-high (375°) until hot. Add mushrooms and garlic; stir-fry 4 minutes.

Add wine; cover and cook 2 minutes. Uncover and cook 2 minutes or until liquid evaporates. Sprinkle mixture with thyme, salt, and pepper; toss well. Serve immediately. Yield: 4 (¾-cup) servings.

PER SERVING: 89 CALORIES (19% FROM FAT)
FAT 1.9G (SATURATED FAT 0.3G)
PROTEIN 4.1G CARBOHYDRATE 13.4G
CHOLESTEROL 0MG SODIUM 156MG

MARINATED PEAS AND MUSHROOMS

6 pearl onions
1 teaspoon olive oil
1 cup shelled fresh English peas
9 small carrots, cut into 3-inch pieces
1½ cups small fresh mushrooms
1½ cups fresh shiitake mushrooms, stems
     removed
12 fresh parsley sprigs
8 small mint leaves
⅔ cup tarragon-flavored vinegar
½ cup water
1 teaspoon mustard seeds
1 teaspoon mixed peppercorns
½ teaspoon salt

Drop onions into a saucepan of boiling water; return to a boil. Drain; rinse under cold water. Drain and peel.

Heat oil in a wok or large nonstick skillet at medium (350°) until hot. Add onions; cook, stirring constantly, 5 minutes. Add peas and carrot; cook, stirring constantly, 5 minutes or until crisp-tender. Remove from heat; stir in mushrooms, parsley, and mint. Spoon vegetable mixture into a shallow dish or glass bowl; set aside.

Combine vinegar and remaining 4 ingredients in a small saucepan; bring to a boil. Pour vinegar mixture over vegetables; cover and marinate in refrigerator at least 2 hours. Serve with a slotted spoon. Yield: 4 (1-cup) servings.

PER SERVING: 96 CALORIES (18% FROM FAT)
FAT 1.9G (SATURATED FAT 0.2G)
PROTEIN 4.3G CARBOHYDRATE 17.9G
CHOLESTEROL 0MG SODIUM 321MG

OKRA-TOMATO-ZUCCHINI STIR-FRY

1 small zucchini
Vegetable cooking spray
1½ cups sliced fresh okra
2 tablespoons chopped onion
1 cup chopped fresh tomato
⅛ teaspoon dried basil
⅛ teaspoon dried thyme
Dash of freshly ground pepper

Cut zucchini in half lengthwise; cut into ¼-inch-thick slices.

Coat a wok or large nonstick skillet with cooking spray; heat at medium-high (375°) until hot. Add zucchini, okra, and onion; stir-fry 4 minutes.

Stir in tomato and remaining ingredients. Cover wok, and cook at low (200°) for 5 minutes or until thoroughly heated, stirring frequently. Yield: 4 (½-cup) servings.

PER SERVING: 31 CALORIES (12% FROM FAT)
FAT 0.4G (SATURATED FAT 0.0G)
PROTEIN 1.5G CARBOHYDRATE 6.3G
CHOLESTEROL 0MG SODIUM 8MG

Okra-Tomato-Zucchini Stir-Fry

Three-Pepper Stir-Fry

THREE-PEPPER STIR-FRY

Vegetable cooking spray
1 medium-size green pepper, cut into very thin strips
1 medium-size sweet red pepper, cut into very thin strips
1 medium-size sweet yellow pepper, cut into very thin strips
¼ cup plus 2 tablespoons sliced green onions
3 tablespoons dry white wine
1½ teaspoons minced fresh basil or ½ teaspoon dried basil
¼ teaspoon dill seeds
¼ teaspoon celery seeds
Fresh basil sprigs (optional)

Coat a wok or large nonstick skillet with cooking spray; heat at medium-high (375°) until hot. Add green pepper and next 7 ingredients; stir-fry 2 to 3 minutes or until pepper is crisp-tender. Garnish with basil sprigs, if desired. Yield: 4 servings.

PER SERVING: 20 CALORIES (23% FROM FAT)
FAT 0.5G (SATURATED FAT 0.1G)
PROTEIN 0.7G CARBOHYDRATE 3.9G
CHOLESTEROL 0MG SODIUM 4MG

MANGO-PEPPER MEDLEY

Vegetable cooking spray
2 teaspoons vegetable oil
1 large green pepper, seeded and cut into thin strips
1 medium-size sweet red pepper, seeded and cut into thin strips
2 teaspoons finely chopped purple onion
¼ cup water
2 tablespoons white wine vinegar
1 teaspoon sugar
½ teaspoon dry mustard
2 cups canned mango slices, drained
2 tablespoons chopped fresh cilantro

Coat a wok or large nonstick skillet with cooking spray; add oil. Heat at medium-high (375°) until hot. Add peppers and onion; stir-fry 1 minute.

Combine water and next 3 ingredients; add to vegetable mixture, and stir-fry 3 minutes. Add mango; stir-fry 1 minute or until thoroughly heated. Transfer to a serving bowl; sprinkle with cilantro. Serve immediately. Yield: 4 (1-cup) servings.

PER SERVING: 132 CALORIES (18% FROM FAT)
FAT 2.6G (SATURATED FAT 0.5G)
PROTEIN 1.4G CARBOHYDRATE 26.2G
CHOLESTEROL 0MG SODIUM 139MG

SPICY PEPPERS AND SNOW PEAS

½ cup dry sherry
3 cups (2- x 1-inch) strips sweet yellow pepper
¼ cup chopped green onions
2 teaspoons minced jalapeño pepper
2 cups (1-inch) diagonally sliced fresh snow pea pods
2 teaspoons sesame seeds, toasted
2 tablespoons low-sodium soy sauce
2 teaspoons honey
1½ teaspoons dark sesame oil
1 teaspoon rice vinegar

Bring sherry to a boil in a wok or large nonstick skillet at medium-high (375°). Add yellow pepper, green onions, and jalapeño pepper; stir-fry 8 minutes or until liquid evaporates and pepper is lightly browned. Add snow peas; stir-fry 1 minute. Remove from heat.

Combine sesame seeds and remaining 4 ingredients. Add to pepper mixture; toss well. Yield: 4 (1-cup) servings.

PER SERVING: 98 CALORIES (28% FROM FAT)
FAT 3.0G (SATURATED FAT 0.4G)
PROTEIN 4.2G CARBOHYDRATE 15.1G
CHOLESTEROL 0MG SODIUM 252MG

CURRIED SNOW PEAS

2 small oranges
¼ teaspoon curry powder
Vegetable cooking spray
½ pound fresh snow pea pods, trimmed
¼ teaspoon sesame seeds

Peel and section oranges over a bowl, reserving juice. Set orange sections aside. Combine reserved juice and curry powder; stir well, and set aside.

Coat a wok or large nonstick skillet with cooking spray; heat at medium-high (375°) until hot. Add snow peas, and stir-fry 2 minutes. Add curry mixture and sesame seeds, stirring well. Reduce heat to medium (350°). Add orange sections, and stir gently. Cook until thoroughly heated, stirring gently. Yield: 4 (½-cup) servings.

PER SERVING: 40 CALORIES (9% FROM FAT)
FAT 0.4G (SATURATED FAT 0.0G)
PROTEIN 1.7G   CARBOHYDRATE 8.0G
CHOLESTEROL 0MG   SODIUM 2MG

SNOW PEA-CARAMBOLA STIR-FRY

¼ pound fresh snow pea pods, trimmed
1 tablespoon reduced-calorie margarine
1 teaspoon peeled, minced gingerroot
1 medium carambola (star fruit), thinly sliced
1 medium-size red pear, cored and thinly sliced
3 tablespoons unsweetened apple juice
¼ teaspoon sugar
¼ teaspoon salt

Cut snow peas in half diagonally; set aside.

Melt margarine in a large nonstick skillet over medium-high heat. Add gingerroot, and stir-fry 1 minute.

Add sliced carambola, and stir-fry 3 minutes. Add reserved snow peas, sliced pear, apple juice, sugar, and salt; stir-fry 3 to 5 additional minutes or until snow peas are crisp-tender.

Transfer mixture to a small serving bowl, and serve immediately. Yield: 4 (½-cup) servings.

PER SERVING: 60 CALORIES (32% FROM FAT)
FAT 2.1G (SATURATED FAT 0.3G)
PROTEIN 1.0G   CARBOHYDRATE 10.5G
CHOLESTEROL 0MG   SODIUM 103MG

PINEAPPLE-GLAZED SUGAR SNAP PEAS

1 (8-ounce) can pineapple chunks in juice, undrained
1 tablespoon brown sugar
2 tablespoons white vinegar
2 tablespoons water
1 teaspoon cornstarch
1 teaspoon low-sodium soy sauce
Vegetable cooking spray
1 teaspoon vegetable oil
1 (8-ounce) package frozen Sugar Snap peas, thawed
¼ cup chopped onion

Drain pineapple, reserving 2 tablespoons juice; set pineapple aside. Combine 2 tablespoons reserved juice, brown sugar, and next 4 ingredients, stirring well. Set aside.

Coat a wok or large nonstick skillet with cooking spray; add oil. Heat at medium-high (375°) until hot. Add Sugar Snap peas and onion. Stir-fry 5 minutes or until crisp-tender.

Add juice mixture to wok. Cook at medium (350°), stirring constantly, 1 minute or until sauce thickens. Stir in pineapple chunks. Serve immediately. Yield: 4 servings.

PER SERVING: 99 CALORIES (15% FROM FAT)
FAT 1.6G (SATURATED FAT 0.2G)
PROTEIN 3.2G   CARBOHYDRATE 18.6G
CHOLESTEROL 0MG   SODIUM 85MG

Pineapple-Glazed Sugar Snap Peas

VEGETABLE STIR-FRY

Olive oil-flavored vegetable cooking spray
1 medium onion, cut into thin wedges
1½ cups julienne-sliced carrot
1½ cups fresh Sugar Snap peas, trimmed
1 cup chopped sweet red pepper
½ cup canned low-sodium chicken broth,
    undiluted
2 tablespoons low-sodium soy sauce
2 teaspoons cornstarch
1 teaspoon sugar
¼ teaspoon ground ginger
⅛ teaspoon ground red pepper

Coat a wok or large nonstick skillet with cooking spray. Heat at medium-high (375°) until hot. Add onion; stir-fry 3 minutes. Add carrot; stir-fry 2 minutes. Add peas and sweet red pepper; stir-fry 4 to 5 minutes or until vegetables are crisp-tender.

Combine chicken broth and remaining 5 ingredients, stirring with a wire whisk until smooth; add to vegetable mixture. Cook, stirring constantly, until mixture is thickened. Yield: 8 (½-cup) servings.

PER SERVING: 42 CALORIES (9% FROM FAT)
FAT 0.4G (SATURATED FAT 0.0G)
PROTEIN 1.5G   CARBOHYDRATE 8.3G
CHOLESTEROL 0MG   SODIUM 111MG

ORIENTAL SPINACH AND VEGETABLES

1 pound fresh spinach
2 tablespoons low-sodium soy sauce, divided
1 teaspoon cornstarch
Vegetable cooking spray
2 teaspoons vegetable oil
1½ cups thinly sliced carrot
1 medium onion, thinly sliced and separated
    into rings
1 clove garlic, minced
1 teaspoon peeled, minced gingerroot
1 (8-ounce) can sliced water chestnuts,
    drained
6 ounces fresh snow pea pods, trimmed

Remove and discard stems from spinach. Wash spinach leaves, and gently pat dry with paper towels. Set spinach aside.

Combine 1 tablespoon soy sauce and cornstarch in a small bowl; stir well, and set aside.

Coat a wok or a large skillet with cooking spray; add oil. Heat at medium-high (375°) until hot. Add carrot, onion, garlic, and gingerroot; stir-fry 2 minutes. Add spinach, water chestnuts, snow peas, and remaining 1 tablespoon soy sauce; stir-fry 5 to 6 minutes or until snow peas are crisp-tender. Add cornstarch mixture to vegetable mixture; cook, stirring constantly, 1 minute or until thickened. Yield: 8 (½-cup) servings.

PER SERVING: 57 CALORIES (24% FROM FAT)
FAT 1.5G (SATURATED FAT 0.3G)
PROTEIN 2.3G   CARBOHYDRATE 9.5G
CHOLESTEROL 0MG   SODIUM 140MG

SPINACH STIR-FRY

Olive oil-flavored vegetable cooking spray
½ teaspoon olive oil
2 cloves garlic, peeled and cut in half
1 pound torn fresh spinach
1 tablespoon fresh lemon juice
⅛ teaspoon salt

Coat a wok or large nonstick skillet with cooking spray; add oil. Heat at medium-high (375°) until hot. Add garlic; stir-fry 3 to 4 minutes or until garlic starts to brown. Add spinach; stir-fry 2 to 3 minutes or just until wilted. Remove and discard garlic. Reduce heat to medium (350°). Add lemon juice and salt; cook 2 to 3 minutes, stirring occasionally. Yield: 2 servings.

PER SERVING: 67 CALORIES (30% FROM FAT)
FAT 2.2G (SATURATED FAT 0.3G)
PROTEIN 6.6G   CARBOHYDRATE 9.1G
CHOLESTEROL 0MG   SODIUM 326MG

GARDEN COMBO

Serve this vegetable medley either on the side or over pasta for a meatless main dish.

1 teaspoon vegetable oil
1 cup sliced onion, separated into rings
1 cup sweet red pepper strips
2 cloves garlic, minced
1¾ cups sliced yellow squash
1¾ cups sliced zucchini
1 cup chopped unpeeled plum tomato
1 tablespoon julienne-sliced fresh basil
½ teaspoon salt-free lemon-pepper seasoning
¼ teaspoon salt
2 tablespoons grated Parmesan cheese

Heat oil in a wok or large nonstick skillet at medium-high (375°). Add onion, red pepper, and garlic; stir-fry 2 minutes. Add yellow squash and zucchini; stir-fry 3 minutes or until vegetables are crisp-tender. Add tomato and next 3 ingredients; cook 1 minute or until thoroughly heated. Remove from heat; sprinkle with Parmesan cheese. Serve immediately. Yield: 5 (1-cup) servings.

PER SERVING: 63 CALORIES (28% FROM FAT)
FAT 2.0G (SATURATED FAT 0.6G)
PROTEIN 3.0G   CARBOHYDRATE 10.1G
CHOLESTEROL 2MG   SODIUM 162MG

Garden Combo

Seasoned Spaghetti Squash

SEASONED SPAGHETTI SQUASH

Parboiling the whole squash for 1 to 2 minutes will make it easier to cut.

1 small spaghetti squash (about 2 pounds)
1 tablespoon reduced-calorie margarine
1 cup chopped onion
1 clove garlic, minced
1 teaspoon dried oregano
½ teaspoon salt
¼ teaspoon pepper

Wash squash; cut in half lengthwise. Remove and discard seeds. Place squash, cut side down, in a Dutch oven; add water to depth of 2 inches. Bring to a boil; cover, reduce heat, and simmer 20 to 25 minutes or until squash is tender.

Drain squash, and cool. Using a fork, remove spaghetti-like strands; set aside, and keep warm. Discard squash shells.

Melt margarine in a large nonstick skillet over medium-high heat. Add onion and garlic; stir-fry just until onion is tender. Add oregano, salt, and pepper; stir well. Add warm squash, and toss gently. Yield: 6 (½-cup) servings.

Note: Squash may be cooked in the microwave. Pierce squash several times with a fork; place on paper towels. Microwave, uncovered, at HIGH 10 to 12 minutes, turning halfway through cooking time. Cut squash lengthwise; discard seeds. Using a fork, remove spaghetti-like strands. Proceed with recipe as directed.

PER SERVING: 44 CALORIES (31% FROM FAT)
FAT 1.5G (SATURATED FAT 0.2G)
PROTEIN 0.9G   CARBOHYDRATE 7.7G
CHOLESTEROL 0MG   SODIUM 228MG

DILLED ZUCCHINI AND SPROUTS

Olive oil-flavored vegetable cooking spray
½ teaspoon olive oil
1 cup julienne-sliced green pepper
2 cloves garlic, minced
2 cups julienne-sliced zucchini
2 cups fresh bean sprouts
½ teaspoon dried dillweed
¼ teaspoon salt
⅛ teaspoon pepper

Coat a wok or large nonstick skillet with cooking spray; add olive oil. Heat at medium-high (375°) until hot. Add green pepper and garlic; stir-fry 5 minutes or until pepper is crisp-tender. Add zucchini, and stir-fry 3 minutes. Stir in bean sprouts and remaining ingredients, and stir-fry 5 minutes or until vegetables are tender. Yield: 5 (½-cup) servings.

PER SERVING: 28 CALORIES (26% FROM FAT)
FAT 0.8G (SATURATED FAT 0.1G)
PROTEIN 1.8G   CARBOHYDRATE 4.9G
CHOLESTEROL 0MG   SODIUM 122MG

Sodium Alert

Be aware that many Asian sauces and condiments are high in sodium. If you are trying to control the sodium in your diet, here are some ways to limit sodium in stir-fries:

• Omit salt in the stir-fry, and do not add salt to the water for cooking rice or noodles.

• Use low-sodium soy sauce instead of the regular version.

• Eliminate monosodium glutamate (MSG) altogether. It is no longer a recommended ingredient, although you may find it listed in some commercial seasoning mixes.

Zucchini Italienne

ZUCCHINI ITALIENNE

Vegetable cooking spray
2½ cups sliced zucchini (about 2 medium)
1¼ cups diced tomato
1½ teaspoons minced fresh basil or ½
    teaspoon dried basil
¾ teaspoon minced fresh oregano or ¼
    teaspoon dried oregano
¼ cup (1 ounce) shredded part-skim
    mozzarella cheese
Fresh basil sprig (optional)

Coat a wok or large nonstick skillet with cooking spray; heat at medium-high (375°) until hot. Add zucchini, and stir-fry 3 to 4 minutes or until crisp-tender. Add tomato, minced basil, and oregano; cook until thoroughly heated. Transfer to a serving dish, and sprinkle with cheese. Garnish with fresh basil sprig, if desired. Yield: 4 (½-cup) servings.

PER SERVING: 42 CALORIES (34% FROM FAT)
FAT 1.6G (SATURATED FAT 0.8G)
PROTEIN 3.1G CARBOHYDRATE 5.0G
CHOLESTEROL 4MG SODIUM 40MG

VEGETABLE CURRY

½ cup no-salt-added tomato juice
½ cup canned vegetable broth, undiluted
1 tablespoon cornstarch
2 teaspoons curry powder
1 teaspoon peeled, minced gingerroot
¼ teaspoon salt
⅛ teaspoon ground red pepper
½ pound fresh green beans
Vegetable cooking spray
1 teaspoon vegetable oil
1 cup diagonally sliced carrot
2 tablespoons water, divided
1 cup fresh broccoli flowerets
½ cup coarsely chopped onion
1 cup coarsely chopped sweet red pepper
1 cup sliced zucchini
1 cup sliced fresh okra

Combine first 7 ingredients; stir until smooth. Set aside. Wash beans; trim ends, and remove strings.

Coat a wok or large nonstick skillet with cooking spray; add oil, and heat at medium-high (375°) until hot. Add beans and carrot; stir-fry 2 minutes. Add 1 tablespoon water, broccoli, and onion; stir-fry 4 minutes. Add remaining 1 tablespoon water, sweet red pepper, zucchini, and okra; stir-fry 4 minutes.

Add tomato juice mixture to wok; cook, stirring constantly, 1 to 2 minutes or until mixture is thickened and bubbly. Yield: 5 (1-cup) servings.

PER SERVING: 72 CALORIES (20% FROM FAT)
FAT 1.6G (SATURATED FAT 0.2G)
PROTEIN 2.7G CARBOHYDRATE 13.7G
CHOLESTEROL 0MG SODIUM 209MG

HOT AND SPICY VEGETABLES
(pictured on page 118)

2 teaspoons cornstarch
2 teaspoons sugar
¼ to ½ teaspoon dried crushed red pepper
½ cup water
¾ pound fresh broccoli
2 teaspoons vegetable oil
1 medium onion, thinly sliced
3 medium carrots, scraped and cut into very
    thin strips
1½ pounds small fresh mushrooms, halved

Combine first 4 ingredients; stir well, and set aside.

Trim off large leaves of broccoli. Remove tough ends of lower stalks, and separate into flowerets. Cut stalks into ¼-inch slices; set aside.

Heat oil in a wok or large nonstick skillet at medium-high (375°) until hot. Add onion; stir-fry 2 minutes. Add broccoli and carrot; stir-fry until crisp-tender. Add mushrooms; stir-fry 2 minutes. Stir in reserved cornstarch mixture; cook, stirring constantly, until thickened. Yield: 8 servings.

PER SERVING: 67 CALORIES (23% FROM FAT)
FAT 1.7G (SATURATED FAT 0.3G)
PROTEIN 3.4G CARBOHYDRATE 11.9G
CHOLESTEROL 0MG SODIUM 24MG

STIR-FRIED ASIAN VEGETABLES

¾ cup canned low-sodium chicken broth
1 tablespoon cornstarch
2 tablespoons low-sodium soy sauce
½ teaspoon sugar
⅛ teaspoon pepper
1 tablespoon vegetable oil
1 cup diagonally sliced carrot
1 cup diagonally sliced celery
½ cup chopped onion
1½ cups snow pea pods, trimmed
1 (15-ounce) can whole baby corn, drained
1 (15-ounce) can whole straw mushrooms,
    drained

Combine first 5 ingredients in a small bowl; mix well, and set aside.

Heat oil in a wok or large nonstick skillet at high (400°). Add carrot, celery, and onion; stir-fry 2 minutes. Add snow peas, corn, and mushrooms; stir-fry 2 minutes. Add broth mixture to vegetable mixture; stir-fry 1 minute or until thickened and bubbly. Yield: 6 (1-cup) servings.

PER SERVING: 119 CALORIES (23% FROM FAT)
FAT 3.0G (SATURATED FAT 0.5G)
PROTEIN 3.8G CARBOHYDRATE 21.6G
CHOLESTEROL 0MG SODIUM 435MG

Stir-Fried Asian Vegetables

INDEX